The
Complete Guide
to Upholstery

The Complete Guide to Upholstery

Stuffed with Step-by-Step Techniques
for Professional Results

Cherry Dobson

St. Martin's Griffin
New York

THE COMPLETE GUIDE TO UPHOLSTERY. Copyright © 2009 by Quarto Inc.
All rights reserved. Printed in China. For information, address St. Martin's Press,
175 Fifth Avenue, New York, N.Y. 10010.
www.stmartins.com

The written instructions, photographs, designs, patterns, and projects in this volume are intended for personal use of the reader and may be reproduced for that purpose only.

Library of Congress Cataloging-in-Publication Data available upon request.

ISBN-13: 978-0-312-38327-5
ISBN-10: 0-312-38327-4

QUAR: TUB

First St. Martin's Press Edition: March 2009

Conceived, designed, and produced by
Quarto Publishing plc
The Old Brewery
6 Blundell Street
London N7 9BH

Project Editor: Ben Hubbard
Art Editor: Jacqueline Palmer
Designer: Louise Downey
Art Director: Caroline Guest
Illustrators: Kuo Kang Chen, John Woodcock
Photographer: Paul Forrester, Simon Pask
Picture research: Sarah Bell

Art Director: Moira Clinch
Publisher: Paul Carslake

Manufactured by SC (Sang Choy) International Pte Ltd., Singapore
Printed in Singapore by Star Standard Industries Pte Ltd

10 9 8 7 6 5 4 3 2 1

Dedication

To the memory of my father Harry Cook, who endowed me with his practical skills, and my late husband Roger, whose spirit has been ever present over my shoulder during the preparation of this guide.

Contents

FOREWORD	**6**
About this book	8
The upholsterer's art	10
TOOLS AND MATERIALS	**12**
Basic tools	14
Webbings and springs	17
Materials	18
Stuffings, fillings, and foam	20
Coverings and linings	22
Textiles	24
Trimmings	30
TECHNIQUES	**32**
Stripping	34
Webbing	40
Springing	46
Working a sprung edge	54
Preparing a burlap base	58
First stuffings	68
Stitching an edge	80
Second stuffings	86
Planning your fabric cuts	92
Attaching new coverings	94
Deep buttoning	98
Vandyking	103
Shallow buttoning	104
Making single and double welt	106
Making box cushions	108
Finishing the chair	112
Close nailing and adding a nail strip	114
TYPES OF FURNITURE	**116**
Dining chairs	118
Stuffed over-seats	120
Armchairs	122
Nursing chairs	132
Wood frames	134
Settees	138
Chaise longues	140
Index	142
Credits	144

Foreword

The restoration and reupholstery of furniture has recently been enjoying a revival. This new appreciation has been fueled by an admiration of traditional quality, the wonderful variety of fabrics available, and the desire of people of all ages and backgrounds to embark upon projects with pleasing and worthwhile objectives.
This guide will help lead you through the basics of the craft, but also introduce you to some of my personal "tips," which come from many years' experience of tackling the "knotty problems" that frequently occur in upholstery. The craft is labor intensive and requires patience and perseverance—but the rewards are wonderful. I hope that this book will be a useful addition to your bookshelf and will encourage you, so that you will both enjoy and take pride in the results.

Acknowledgments

To my mother for her love and patience when I have been engrossed in the "book." To my many friends who have been so supportive, especially to Peter for his diligent proof reading, and to Pat for providing the food. Not forgetting the students I have met over the past 25 years. Without them and their chairs, I would never have learned so much. Hopefully this book will be a reminder to all of them of the techniques I have taught them.

About this book

This book is a complete course in upholstering furniture, including tooling up, selecting stuffings and outer textiles, techniques, and cutting plans.

Tools and materials

(pages 12–31)

Starting with the basic tools, this section gives an overview of the equipment you'll need, including springs, stuffings, and textiles.

Identification guide
Identifies and illustrates the upholsterer's kit.

Techniques

(pages 33–115)

Most of the techniques are demonstrated on chairs but the same principles can be applied to larger pieces of furniture in need of upholstery.

Tools and materials listing
At each stage, the tools and materials you will need are listed.

Supplementary diagrams
Diagrams supplement the photographic information.

About this book   9

Types of furniture

This part identifies what lies beneath the "skin" of different types of furniture. No two pieces of furniture are identical: use this section as a guide to plan how to measure your project and how to cut fabric to minimize the quantity you have to buy. In many cases, cutting plans are provided for both plain and patterned fabric.

Cross references
The techniques required to upholster a similar piece are listed here.

Taking measurements
Diagram illustrates the important measurements needed to plan how much upholstery fabric to purchase.

Key
In this section, the following abbreviations are used. Here, imperial measurements precede metric measurements.

I = inner
O = outer
A = arm
B = back
Shaded area = waste or welt

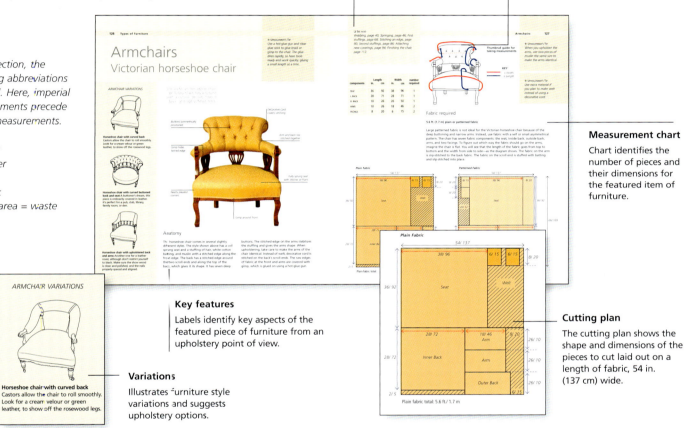

Measurement chart
Chart identifies the number of pieces and their dimensions for the featured item of furniture.

Key features
Labels identify key aspects of the featured piece of furniture from an upholstery point of view.

Cutting plan
The cutting plan shows the shape and dimensions of the pieces to cut laid out on a length of fabric, 54 in. (137 cm) wide.

Variations
Illustrates furniture style variations and suggests upholstery options.

Upholsterer's Order of Work

1. Find a piece of furniture to upholster. If you are a beginner choose something simple, such as a chair with a drop-in seat.

2. Strip the furniture (pages 34–39), making a note of the materials that have been used and how they were applied.

3. Apply the webbing (pages 40–45) to create a platform for the stuffings.

4. Check the condition of the springs and either reuse or replace them (pages 46–57).

5. Add burlap to cover the springs (pages 58–67).

6. Apply the first layer of stuffing (pages 68–79).

7. Apply a stitched edge for shape retention (pages 80–85).

8. Apply a second stuffing of hair (pages 86–91).

9. Measure and cut the new coverings and apply (pages 92–97).

10. Add buttoning if required (pages 98–102 and 104–105).

11. Add the finishing touches, such as welt, braid, gimp and studs (pages 112–115).

12. Finish the piece with lining underneath the chair to conceal the workings of the upholstery (page 113).

The upholsterer's art

Traditional methods of upholstery are still used today despite the invention of synthetic fibers and a number of mechanical labor-saving devices. Upholstery is a skilled craft requiring judgment and dexterity and every piece of furniture needs to be approached differently. The stuffing is built up gradually following the contours of the frame and the upholsterer has to judge whether the shape and height look and feel right.

An ornate French armchair, from the reign of Louis XVI. With upholstered seat, back, and arm rests. This is the work of a famous Paris-based master upholsterer called Georges Jacob (1739–1814).

Early upholstery was rudimentary. Girthweb—the type of webbing used for making saddle girths—was woven across the frame and tacked at the edges. In France it was close-woven, but elsewhere there were large gaps between the girths. The webbing was then covered with a piece of burlap or coarse sackcloth and some form of padding was piled on, either feathers, wool, animal hair, or vegetable matter such as straw, chaff, rushes or dried grasses and leaves. Occasionally the padding was roughly secured with bridle ties before the top cover was nailed on. The backs of chairs were usually stuffed with washed and curled horsehair, which was more expensive, stitched onto a linen or canvas backing. After about 1660 horsehair was used to a much greater extent and the front and sometimes the sides of the seats, which received the greatest wear, were strengthened with an extra band of stuffing sewn into a roll of burlap or canvas.

Additional layers of fabric, usually wadding or linen, were placed between the horsehair and the top cover to prevent the hair from working its way through the fine fabric above. Some chairs had loose cushions filled with down or feathers.

In the eighteenth century these techniques were refined, and complicated curved and straight-edged upholstery was carefully molded by more precise stuffing and stitching. Often there were two layers of stuffing on the seat—one thin layer of horsehair above a thicker layer of cheap vegetable fiber. Sometimes the padding was held in place with stitching or with regularly spaced ties that gave the surface of the upholstery a slightly indented pattern. This is now called shallow buttoning or tufting because silk tufts and not buttons were used as a decorative finish to each tie. In France, tufting was described as capitonné. Buttons did not replace the ties until the end of the eighteenth century. Until the middle of the eighteenth century, the upholstery of a chair or sofa was its most important part and often cost more in materials and workmanship than the frame. Consequently the upholsterer, or "upholder," was held in high esteem. In France the two crafts of tapissier (upholsterer) and menuisier (chair maker), were kept entirely separate.

The upholsterer often supplied all the textile furnishings of a house, from the elaborate wall hangings and curtains down to simple pillows and mattresses. As an interior designer, advising his clients on their choice and arrangement of furnishings, he probably had a greater influence on the final appearance of a house than the architect who designed it. (Most upholsterers were also undertakers and supplied the accessories that decorated the funeral cortège and the elaborate black drapes and ornaments that decorated a house during mourning.)

A modern armchair with foam padded seat and back.

Seats get more comfortable

Deep buttoning resulted from the widespread use of the coiled spring after 1820, which greatly deepened the padding. This springing was the only major advance in upholstery technique for over a century. The addition of a layer of springs underneath the layers of stuffing allowed the upholstery to move slightly and therefore made it more comfortable. The backs as well as the seats were often sprung and the thicker stuffing needed to cover the springs was prevented from slipping by the deep-set buttons. The resulting pleating of the material became a decorative feature and buttoning sometimes appeared on the arms too, though they were not always themselves sprung.

At first, springs were attached at the bottom to wooden planks, i.e. similar to modern ready-made wood and metal sprung units, which simply slot into the frame. These were soon replaced by more flexible webbing.

Between 1650 and 1800, horsehair was used for the padding, but as it became more expensive, other materials were used to pad it out. These have included coconut fiber, known as coir or kerly fiber, various coarse grasses and leaves, cotton, rags and wool waste, and even wood chippings. The 20th century saw the introduction of rubber webbing, staple guns, latex, and polyurethane foam.

Tools and Materials

Tools can be purchased through a local supplier or over the Internet. Using the correct tools ensures that each job is done efficiently and professionally. Equally important are the textiles you choose: whether you are going classic or contemporary, buy a textile that combines beauty and quality. You want to create pieces that can be admired and used. The examples here give an idea of what professional upholsterers can achieve.

Basic tools

As a beginner you will need the basic tools to strip your project of its coverings, tacks, and staples. But before this you must consider your workspace. Take into account the area you work in including the walls. Develop a workroom plan so you have enough space to lay out and cut fabric as well as somewhere to store your materials. You will also need to have your furniture on saw horses or an adjustable bench at the correct height for you to work comfortably. Make sure you have an adjustable chair to minimize backache.

The following pages illustrate the tools and equipment you will need as a beginner, but also tools and machinery for professional upholsterers. Many upholstery tools are the same as they were a century ago, although today they are available in different shapes and sizes. It is up to the upholsterer to decide which tools they find the most useful, as most people have tools they favor and others they seldom use. The basic tools that you will need in your tool box, are: a wooden mallet, a ripping chisel, a tack- or staple-remover, pincers, sharp scissors, a webbing stretcher, a magnetic hammer, regulators, a tape measure, needles, pins, and skewers. A more experienced or professional upholsterer may also need: an industrial sewing machine, a buttoning machine, a glue gun, and an electric or pneumatic stapler.

Finding and accessing furniture

Furniture that is suitable for renovation can come from a variety of sources. The auction room, antique shop, or eBay are the most obvious places, but usually the amateur begins with a piece they already own. Before buying furniture to upholster, examine it for woodworm (small bore holes in the wood) to check the frame is solid. The shape and style of the chair usually indicate its age and quality, although faults can be hidden under a layer of upholstery. Normally, a good quality chair is made from a hardwood like mahogany, walnut, or rosewood, which can be seen on the legs or any other show wood on the chair. The shape of the chair legs is also a telling feature—they should be substantial, and not spindly in appearance. The back legs should be made from the same wood as the front, and have an outward or ogee (double) curve. Castors should be made from brass, with china or brass wheels.

Tools: the basic kit

1. A wooden mallet is used in conjunction with a ripping chisel to remove tacks. Use a hickory mallet or a barrel-shaped hickory mallet. Do not strike the chisel with a metal hammer because it could damage its handle.

2. A ripping chisel has either a straight (a) or cranked (b) shaft and is used to lever out tacks. It is used in conjunction with a wooden mallet. Do not use a sharp-edged chisel as you will damage its sharp end when levering out the tacks.

3. A tack remover is used to remove tacks and dome-headed decorative nails used on leather upholstery. It is particularly useful for removing temporary tacks when adjusting the tension of fabrics. Removers may have wooden (a) or plastic (b) handles.

4. Magnetic hammers come in several types—the most popular is the two-headed hammer (a and b) with a magnetic head at one end for picking up and holding tacks, and a larger head at the other end for hammering. A hammer with a rubber end (c) is for hammering tacks into soft or fragile woods.

5. A slot and peg webbing stretcher is used to stretch the webbing tightly over the chair frame. As an alternative use a gooseneck webbing stretcher, which catches the webbing close to the frame.

6. Staple removers come in many types. The blade puller (a) is best for removing staples from fabric and soft wood; and the pronged-end types (b and c) are better for prising staples from hard woods.

7. Sharp scissors are a must. Keep two pairs—a general pair for cutting twine, rubberized hair, and batting, and the other solely for fabrics. Scissors should be a minimum length of 8 in. (20 cm) for trimming; 10 in. (25 cm—or more depending on the size of your hands) for cutting the fabric. It is essential that the fabric scissors have sharp tips so that cuts can be made accurately.

8. Pincers are needed to remove tacks that have lost their heads. They can also be used to pull out stray staples, or remove the nibs of staples that break off.

9. Staple guns vary from the flat-bedded hand-tacker, to the preferable pneumatic or electric gun with a nozzle. Make sure you use the gun's correct-sized staple. The gun should be able to fire staples of the following lengths: 3/16 in. (5 mm); 3/8 in. (10 mm); 1/2 in. (13 mm).

※ **Upholsterer's Tip**
Don't buy cheap scissors—buy the best quality you can afford. Because they will be used in your workroom for a variety of cutting and trimming tasks, it is essential that you keep your scissors sharp and in good condition. You will need a minimum length of 8 in. (20 cm) scissors for trimming, and 10 in. (25 cm) scissors for cutting the fabric.

16 Tools and materials

Tools: the basic kit continued

1. Regulators come in several lengths, with a sharp point at one end and a blunt end at the other. The longer length—the 8 in. or 10 in. (20 cm or 25 cm)—is used for distributing hair evenly under muslin, and the shorter 6 in. (15 cm) is very useful for applying top fabric, because the blunt end helps form neat pleats and tucks.

2. Double-pointed needles are used with twine to form a stitched edge. Needles with a bayonet tip are used when a cutting edge on the needle is required.

3. Skewers are available in two lengths: 3 in. (7.5 cm), and 4 in. (10 cm). They are used for holding fabric in place before it is sewed or tacked down. Pins are available in 1 in. (2.5 cm) lengths, and are also used for holding fabric in place.

4. Large curved needles are used for attaching springs and sewing bridles into burlap. The smaller 3 in. (7.5 cm) curved needles are used for slip-stitching top fabric; and the larger 4 in. (10 cm), or 5 in. (12.5 cm) curved needles for any stitching involving heavier fabrics, such as burlap.

5. A tape measure and yardstick (or meterstick) are used for measuring the chair and estimating how much fabric is required. A soft tape measure, shown here, is used for measuring the fabric components on chairs, and a yardstick is used for measuring and marking fabric prior to cutting.

6. Wax chalk (not shown) for marking fabric for cutting. Wax chalk does not rub off too easily.

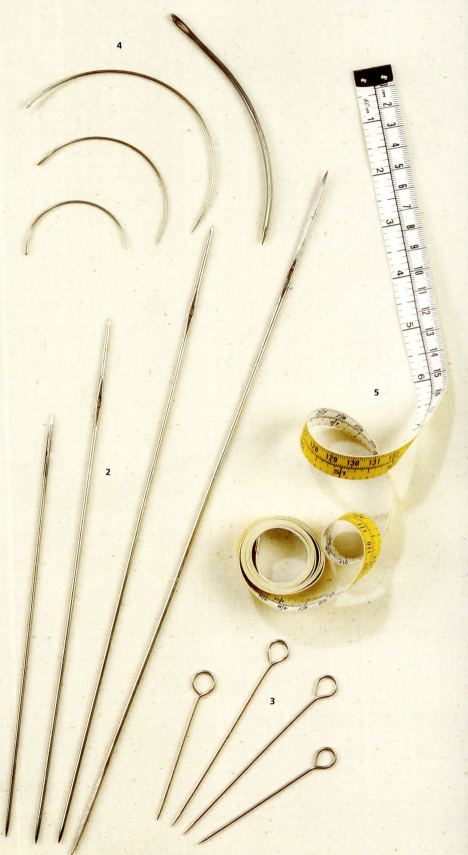

Webbings and springs

Webbing is used as the foundation for furniture. A strong seat requires a strong base, with properly spaced webbing that will even the weight and diameter of the springs used. There are several types of webbing made from jute, linen, cotton or rubber (called Pirelli and elastic webbing). When reupholstering, use webbing similar to that originally used on the chair. Stretch the webbing across your frame using a webbing stretcher to form a sound base for the subsequent materials. Always use good quality webbing and never reuse the old webbing, which will almost certainly be past its sell-by-date. Springs are an integral part of traditional upholstery, and while not all seating must be sprung, springs do add depth and comfort that you don't always get with just padding and foam. Your choice of spring will depend on the piece you are upholstering. If you replace springs, use the same type used in the original upholstery.

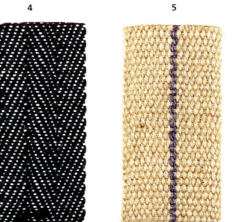

Springs

1. Tension springs are more commonly used on fireside chairs and are fixed with clips or hooked into a webbing or metal plate with eyelet holes. The springs should be stretched across the frame of the chair and measure 1 in. (2.5 cm) less than the width of the frame.

2. Coil springs are used in traditional chairs and come in a variety of heights and gauges. The firmer No. 9 or No. 10 springs are used on the seat, and the softer No. 12 springs are used for the backs. The number of springs used depends on the size of the seat. A dining chair, for example, would have four 5 in. (12.5 cm) No. 10 gauge springs, whereas a large armchair would have nine 7 in. or 8 in. (17 cm or 20 cm) No. 9 springs.

3. Serpentine springs are used for all modern upholstery. They are attached by clips across the frame of the chair from back to front and, for the professional upholsterer, are a quick and easy type of spring to apply.

Webbing

4. Black and white webbing (with a Herringbone pattern) is the best quality but also the most expensive. It usually comes in a 2 in. (5 cm) width, and is used on traditional chairs.

5. Jute is the next best alternative to black and white and is the webbing most commonly used.

6. Pirelli webbing is used on modern chairs to replace tens on or serpentine springs, and to form a base for a seat upholstered with foam or rubberized hair. It is stretched across the chair frame and held in place with either clips or staples.

7. Elastic webbing, also called heavy rubberized elastic webbing, is used as an alternative to Pirelli webbbing.

Materials

Materials and fabrics are anchored and attached to furniture with tacks, staples, or gimp pins, using a hammer or staple gun. Tacks can be bought in boxes of 3½ oz. (100 gm), or small packets and staples in boxes of 2,500.

1. Laid cord is used for lashing down springs. It has very little stretch and is made from hemp, flax and jute. It is available in 9 oz. (250 gm) or 18 oz. (500 gm) balls.

2. Twines and cords are made from flax, jute and hemp and come in graded sizes 1 to 4. Waxed twines made from flax are stronger than those made from other fibers, and are recommended for all upholstery work. Nylon twine is cheap and good for buttoning, and can be used instead of laid cord to tie down springs. Twines come in ½ lb (250 gm) balls. No. 3 is a good all round twine to use.

3. Piping/welt cord is commonly made from cotton and makes piping/welt. It can be natural or pre-shrunk. Use the pre-shrunk type to make cushions that will be washed. The thickness of the piping cord depends on the type of fabric used.

4. Staples come in sizes similar to the tacks above. Longer staples are used for webbing and burlap, and short ones for muslin and top covers.

5. Cut or blue tacks come in two basic types: fine and improved. Fine tacks have a small head and are used on fabrics with a close-weave, such as top fabric or muslin. Improved tacks have larger heads and are used on loose-weave fabrics such as webbing, burlap, and scrim. They come in the following lengths: ⅝ in. (16 mm) improved tacks for webbing, and for anchoring spring ties; ⅝ in. (16 mm) fine tacks for webbing where the wood is liable to split; ½ in. (13 mm) improved for burlap; ½ in. (13 mm) fine tacks for tacking through thicker layers of cloth; ⅜ in. (10 mm) improved tacks for attaching scrim when constructing a stitched edge; and ⅜ in. (10 mm) fine tacks for attaching muslin and top coverings.

6. Decorative nails are patterned with a brass or bronze finish. They can also be colored and are used individually to anchor the top fabric.

7. Nail strips are used to cover the cut edges of leather or vinyl furniture.

8. Domed nails are plain with either a brass or bronze finish and are used for close nailing or attaching a nail strip.

Gimp pins (not shown) are small, fine, colored tacks, which come in ⅜ in. (10 mm) and ½ in. (13 mm), and are used to attach braid and gimp. They can also be used as a final fixing to coordinate with the top fabric.

Stuffings, fillings, and foam

When a piece of furniture is stripped, its stuffings are revealed. Throw away the battings, but keep the hair and fiber, unless the strands of hair have broken into small pieces. The hair can be placed in a pillowcase and washed by hand or in a machine. You can use hair from an old mattress if it is of good quality. When purchasing stuffings, it is worth buying the best you can afford.

There are several types of animal hair available to buy, ranging from the common hog- and horse-hair, to the more expensive white cattle tail. Ginger coir and black fiber are very good alternatives and much cheaper. All of these are available to buy from upholstery suppliers in 28 lb. (13 kg) bags. Whatever type you choose to use, hair needs to be covered with batting to make a smooth surface and prevent the strands working their way through the top cover.

There are three main types of batting: white cotton batting, blue wool, and polyester batting. Polyester batting is usually used on top of white cotton batting to make an even, smooth finish; on top of foam as a protective cover; or as a lining, before the finishing fabric is attached to the outside arms and back. It is available in several thicknesses and widths, and rolls vary in length between 33 ft (10 m) and 164 ft (50 m). Modern fillings are foam and rubberized hair. Rubberized hair looks a little like horse hair, but strands are coated with rubber latex and bonded together, almost to the consistency of a foam sheet. It is available in 1 in. (2.5 cm) and 2 in. (5 cm) thick sheets, in sizes 36 in. (92 cm) by 72 in. (183 cm). Foam is found on most modern chairs, settees, and headboards and is available in varying grades and thicknesses depending on its use. A good supplier will help advise on which type is best for your project. It is not a cheap option for stuffing, however—the price of foam 2 in. (5 cm) thick is twice the price of that 1 in. (2.5 cm) thick.

Types of stuffings

1. Black fiber is made from shredded leaves that are curled and dyed, and is cheaper than animal hair, although the dye does come off on your hands. Black fiber is used as a first stuffing on chairs and settees and is useful in forming a stitched edge.

2. Animal hair is available to buy in burlap sacks, although it is expensive. It comes in varying qualities but the cheapest one is fine to use. It is used for a first stuffing on drop-in seats, or pincushion seats where there is only one stuffing—or as a second stuffing on other furniture.

3. Ginger coir or coconut fiber is also used as a first stuffing and is useful for forming a stitched edge.

4. Rubberized hair is a good alternative to foam, hair, or coir stuffing on chair seats or backs. It is a good substitute for hair or foam stuffing and is fire retardant. It is easily molded and provides a more traditional feel than foam stuffing. Weight: 36 oz. (1150 gm), size 72 in. x 36 in. (183 cm x 92 cm) Thickness: 1 in. (2.5 cm) or 2 in. (5 cm).

5. Cotton batting is also known as white cotton batting. It is made from pure new cotton that has been layered. There are two weights available, the thinner one is suitable for general upholstery. Fire-retardant battings are also available. The two weights are: 26.5 oz. (750 gm), width 27 in. (68 cm), length 19 yd (17.5 m); 42.3 oz. (1200 gm), width 27 in. (68 cm), length 11.9 yd (11 m). This batting is used to cover hair, coir, or fiber to make a smooth finish and to prevent the hair working through the top cover. It is also used on its own as a pad for simple upholstery.

6. Woollen batting/blue batting comes in two types: layered or needled. It is made from woollen waste, which is woven together. The layered type falls apart easily and is not recommended, but the needled type is strong and useful for covering rubberized hair followed by a covering of white cotton batting. It is also used as a covering for springs in sprung cushions.

7. Skin batting is a thin batting with a cellulose surface. It is used as an additional covering to white cotton batting and provides a very smooth finish. Skin batting is available in 32's and 52's. (no-one seems to know what these numbers relate to). 32's: width 18 in. (46 cm), length 21.5 yd (20 m); 52's: width 18 in. (46 cm) 10.8 yd (10 m).

8. Polyester batting is used as an additional covering for white cotton batting to give a smooth and luxurious feel to the upholstery. It can also be used on the outside of chairs, as batting between the burlap and top fabric. It is available in 2 widths: 27 in. (69 cm), or 54 in. (137 cm); and comes in various thicknesses from 2.5 oz. (70 gm) to 16 oz. (475 gm). The thinnest type is adequate for most upholstery, and the thicker one is normally used only for cushion interiors.

9. Foam (left) comes in different grades and thicknesses, as chip foam and also as latex, which is more expensive. It is available in large sheets or in pieces cut to the exact size and shape required. When using foam, consider its use and how it will be supported in the frame, and always cover it with a protective layer, like stockinette or polyester batting. Otherwise the millions of small holes in the foam can pluck the threads of the finishing fabric. All foams sold in US are fire resistant.

Feathers (not shown) are used as a cushion filler. The feathers can be mixed with down to form a more deluxe filling and come in 55 lb. (25 kg) sacks. Feather cushions can be custom-made, which is preferable, as stuffing a cushion with feathers can prove both difficult and messy.

9

Pincore latex   Reconstituted chip   Common foam

Coverings and linings

There are many different fabrics used when recovering traditional furniture. As illustrated, start with the burlap base and work your way through the layers to build a strong foundation for the proper sequence of coverings and linings.

1 & 2. Burlap is used on top of webbing or springs to act as a base for the hair stuffing, and can be found on traditional or modern pieces of furniture. Burlap is available in three different weights—7.5 oz. (213 gm), 10 oz. (273 gm), and 12 oz. (366 gm)—and is usually 72 in. (18.3 m) wide. The 12 oz. (366 gm) is the best quality and should be used at all times if available.

3 & 4. Scrim is another form of burlap that is like cheesecloth—it has a very loose and airy weave, and is often used for cheap curtains. It is used when a second stuffing and a stitched edge are required on a chair. The evenness of its weave makes stitching an edge easier. It is available in No. 2 or No. 7. qualities. No. 2 is the thickest, with a higher number of yarns to the inch. No. 7 is a looser weave cloth and is used similarly to the No. 2, but is easier to use where the frame has a curve. Both of these scrims are available in a 72 in. (183 cm) width. A superior quality scrim is made from linen—this only comes in a 36 in. (92 cm) width.

5. Muslin (sometimes known as cotton duck) is used to cover and tighten the stuffings that have been applied to a chair. Use muslin underneath a top fabric as it takes the strain before the top fabric is applied. Muslin will also hold the stuffing in place if the cover needs to be changed. Use good quality muslin where possible and take care if it has been treated for fire retardancy, as the fabric can be very brittle and easy to tear. It is often better to use an untreated muslin and then a barrier cloth on top to conform to fire retardancy requirements.

6 & 7. Decking is a strong cloth that comes in various colors and is used on seats underneath loose cushions. However, this makes the cushion non-reversible. In its black form it is used on the underneath of chairs to neaten and act as a dust barrier.

8. Down-proof ticking is a strong cotton fabric used to make cushion pads. It is wax-proofed to prevent feathers and down working their way through the fabric.

9. Blue and white ticking is also used for making cushion interiors and traditionally is a twill weave and blue and white.

10. Stockinette is a knitted fabric that comes in rolls, and is used for covering foam cushions. It is easy to apply although the raw edges at the ends of the cushion need to be overlocked.

Coverings and linings 23

5 6 7 8 9 10

Textiles

There are a number of different textiles to choose from when upholstering a piece of furniture. Your choice of textile will depend on a number of factors—primarily the piece of furniture you are upholstering, but also its use, the room it is going into, and of course your own personal style preferences. Most people know what they like when they see it. But if you take a minute to learn how to define your style preferences, you'll be more likely to find exactly the furnishings you're looking for.

CHOOSING A STYLE

"Style" is a very personal thing. You may love the smooth, sleek lines of contemporary pieces, or you may prefer the traditional charm of furnishings from the 18th century. That's the beauty of home furnishings—there's so much to choose from that it's easy to find the pieces that express your unique style.

It is helpful to know the basic style category you're looking for; it gives you a great place to start. To help you focus in on a "look," browse through your favorite magazines to find pieces or entire rooms that appeal to you. Tear out the pages and take them with you when you shop. Whether it's a sofa, loveseat, chair, or ottoman, upholstered furniture usually falls into one of the following main style categories:

Traditional
This term refers to that designed with a deliberate adherence to the past. It is by far the largest of the style categories, with a dozen or more sub-categories ranging from Italian Renaissance to Louis XV or Queen Anne, and Chippendale to Art Deco. Traditional styles are more conservative—perhaps even formal—and feature a wealth of elegant details, such as symmetrical designs, graceful carved curves, rich and mellow colors, dark polished woods like cherry and mahogany, and fine upholstery. Think of European antiques, wingback chairs, camelback sofas, damask, jacquard and chintz fabric covers, and Oriental influences. These are good examples of what "traditional" styling is all about.

Velvet, chenille, mohair, or maybe even corduroy, these plush fabrics are inviting and long-wearing.

Transitional
These designs blend influences from a variety of old and new style categories. As a result, the overall look is much more up-to-date than pure traditional styles. Transitional designs, since they usually incorporate both traditional and contemporary elements, are more versatile with regard to interior decorating. Furnishings with transitional styling are easy to coordinate, creating a casual, easy-going look. These styles are more understated, and cater to today's laid-back lifestyles. This is the world of overstuffed sofas, easy-care "performance" fabrics, solid colors, and lighter-finish woods that will help you create warm, relaxed interiors that favor neutral colors and soft textures, and make for an inviting look. Picture a loft apartment— light and airy, high ceilings, sleek furniture designs upholstered in neutrals, with artwork, collectables, pillows, and cushions bringing in bright color splashes.

The cranberry stripe at the bottom of this bold design will add color and warmth to an otherwise neutral room.

Contemporary

The term contemporary covers several styles of furniture that were developed in the latter half of the twentieth century. It's not "modern," but it is an updated look with sleek, rounded lines, and clean, crisp shapes. Contemporary is considered to be a fashion-forward, upscale design look that favors simplicity and a minimalist approach—the focus is on function and efficiency. Fabrics lean toward textures and weaves in solids, stripes, and prints. Colors may be neutral, or bold with striking patterns. Leather is a popular upholstery choice for contemporary designs. (Accessories may lean toward metal and glass.)

One of today's most popular upholstery looks is "casual contemporary." It still features lean lines and strong silhouettes, but is much more relaxed, allowing a warmer, more comfortable look.

This polka dot fabric would go well on a Morris chair with a leather seat.

If you're having difficulty figuring out which style is right one for you, don't despair. Lots of folks are "hybrids" when it comes to decorating preferences. When designing a hybrid room, a good way to compromise is to pick a dominant style and then add accent pieces and accessories in a different style. Remember that the number one rule in decorating is: if you like it, it's right. Mix and match, and express yourself.

Remember that fabric "grade" is not an indication of quality or durability, it's just an indicator of how expensive the fabric is to make. Read the details on the fabric label attached to your swatch and make your decision accordingly.

Regardless of color, fiber, thread count, or grade, upholstery fabrics should always be chosen to serve your needs, whether they be fashionable or practical. There are countless choices to be made, so don't settle for anything you're not in love with. Most importantly, be sure to pick a fabric that you can truly live with. And, if you grow tired of it in a few years, remember that virtually all upholstered furniture can be re-covered.

Eclectic

Eclectic interiors are highly individualized and feature a diverse mix of compatible styles. For example, an antique armoire might be paired with a contemporary sofa and chair, with occasional tables that are similar, but don't match. Accents might include objects collected from around the world, unusual artwork, or pieces with whimsical or sentimental value. In eclectic room designs, furniture and textured fabric covers typically cross styles and periods, while color is often the common denominator. True eclectic style can be as distinctive and beautiful as any other category.

Soft colors, like the duck egg blue in this floral design, are ideal for neutral schemes.

Slipcover

Also known as the "slipcover look," this style has a tailored cover that slips on and off for a comfortable, lived-in look (see photo, right). Slipcover styles enable you to change the look of an entire room simply by changing your furniture covers. "True" slipcovers come all the way off for dry cleaning or spot cleaning.

HOW TO CHOOSE AN UPHOLSTERY FABRIC

Nothing has a greater effect on the look of upholstered furniture than the fabric. It is the most visible indicator of both fashion and quality, but also the part of an upholstered piece to show soil and wear fastest. When selecting fabric, you must know what to look for and what questions to ask. With some basic considerations, you'll be able to recognize the differences between fabric types.

STYLE: The fabric should be appropriate to the style and character of the piece it is covering. A traditional frame will usually look best with a more traditional fabric style. Consider the scale of the pattern—this should be appropriate to the size of the room. As a rule, large repeating patterns look better in larger rooms. Also consider whether the fabric color is cool or warm, and be sure it fits the "mood" of the room it will go into.

FADE RESISTANCE: Will your furniture be exposed to constant direct sunlight? To reduce the chances of fading, see if your choices include fabrics that are sunlight resistant. Here's where the synthetics make a very loud case for textiles that aren't just for boats any more!

DURABILITY: Will the furniture be in an area of the house where there is heavy traffic? Pieces subject to daily heavy wear need to be covered in tightly woven, tough, and durable fabrics. Generally speaking, fabrics that have their pattern "woven in" wear better than printed fabrics.

COLOR: This is probably the most influential factor when selecting a fabric, but a specific color may not be the best choice for durability and stain resistance. If your household has small children and/or pets, you're probably better off choosing a color that won't show dirt easily.

TAILORING: Fabric covers should be pulled tightly and contain no snags, unwanted tucks or dimples. Checked and plaid patterns should always be aligned and matched.

FORM AND FIBER: When shopping for fabrics, you'll discover a vast array of different patterns, textures, thread counts, and fiber contents from which to select. But your choice will come down to natural fabrics, synthetics, or a mixture of the two. Following is a rundown of some of your options:

NATURAL FABRICS

COTTON—This natural fiber provides good resistance to wear, fading, and pilling, but is less resistant to soiling and wrinkling. Surface treatments and blending with other fibers often compensate for these weaknesses. Durability and suitability for use will depend on the weave and finish of the fabric: damask weaves are formal, while canvas weaves such as duck and sailcloth are more casual and durable. Cotton is absorbent and feels cool against the skin in warm climates. Heavier weight cottons such as denims wear well, while polished ones, such as chintz, tend to weaken and split in just a few years.

COTTON BLENDS—Depending on the weave, cotton blends tend to be sturdy, family-friendly fabrics. For everyday use, it's a good idea to apply a stain-resistant finish (or look for fabrics which have already been treated, i.e. "Scotchguard").

LEATHER—Perhaps the best all-around upholstery fabric ever! Even though it can be expensive, leather may be a wonderfully rugged choice for your particular project. This tough material comes in many colors and finishes, and develops more softness and character with age. Leather is very forgiving, and easy to clean and maintain. When buying leather for upholstery, go to a reputable hide supplier. If you must, buy "splits", but you may be sorely disappointed in the quality and durability of the leather.

SILK—This beautiful, delicate fabric is suitable for adult areas, such as formal living rooms or bedrooms. It must be professionally cleaned if soiled. For successful upholstery use, silk must be "cotton backed"—this is an additional process done by a lamination service before the fabric is cut and sewn. If you do select silk for your upholstery/drapery project, do not place the furniture in an unprotected sunny location—silk will last for a very long time, but the direct sun will cause it to rot in a few short years.

WOOL—Sturdy and durable, wool and wool blends offer good resistance to pilling, fading, wrinkling, and soiling. Generally, wool is blended with a synthetic fiber to make it easier to clean. Blends can be spot-cleaned when necessary.

SYNTHETICS

ACETATE—Developed as imitation silk, this fabric resists mildew, pilling, and shrinking, but is not a good choice for furniture that will get everyday use.

ACRYLIC—This fabric was developed as imitation wool and resists wear, wrinkling, soiling, and fading. Better quality acrylics are manufactured to resist pilling.

MICROFIBER—This term is used to describe a new category of upholstery fabrics with a velvety, suede-like surface, also known as faux suede. Made from ultra fine polyester fibers, microfiber fabrics are durable and pleasant to the touch. These fabrics are of excellent value, durability, and cleanability.

NYLON—Rarely used alone, nylon is usually blended with other fibers to make it one of the strongest upholstery fabrics. It is very resilient; in a blend it helps eliminate the crushing of napped fabrics, such as velvet and chenilles. It doesn't readily soil or wrinkle, but it does tend to fade and pill.

OLEFIN—A popular, durable choice for furniture likely to receive heavy wear: "bullet proof" comes to mind when thinking of this textile. Contract grade fabrics very often use olefin for long-range projects.

POLYESTER—An attractive choice, rarely used alone in upholstery, polyester is blended with other fibers to add wrinkle resistance, eliminate crushing of napped fabrics (velvets, chenilles), and reduce fading. It neither stretches nor shrinks.

RAYON—Developed as an imitation silk, linen, and cotton, rayon is durable, however, it does wrinkle. Recent advances have made high-quality rayon very practical for upholstery.

VINYL—Easy care and less expensive than leather, vinyls are ideal for busy family living and dining/eating areas, but remember: durability depends on quality.

Fabric families

1. Linen: twice as strong as cotton, and second in strength to silk, linen is an extremely durable natural fiber. However, it is not the obvious choice for the upholsterer, as it lacks the elasticity of cotton blends, is difficult to manipulate, and wrinkles easily. These samples are 100 percent linen, dry clean only, shown here in raspberry and sable.

2, 3, 4, 5, 6. Cotton blend: a cotton blend can consist of various different fiber types, in varying quantities, but a good quality cotton blend will advertise cotton as its principal ingredient. The blends here range from 45 percent cotton, 45 percent linen, 15 percent nylon (top left), to 60 percent cotton, 40 percent modacrylic (center right), to the less reliable 65 percent viscose, 18 percent cotton, 15 percent linen, 2 percent silk (far left).

7. Velvet blend: dense and heavy, velvet is very difficult to wash, so use a sensitive dry clean only. Rayon, cotton, and polyester are common to most blends, but ideally velvet should be made from silk. A small percentage of Lycra is sometimes added to give stretch. The sample colors shown here are: (from left to right) eggplant, off white, cranberry, and biscuit.

8. Polyester: 100 percent polyester (as shown here in gold, brown and natural) is not suitable for upholstery as it resists shrinking and stretching. However, blended with other fibers, polyester is the perfect upholsterer's fabric as it is easy to clean and does not fade.

9. Faux suede: faux suede is a type of leather with a napped finish. Soft yet pliable, suede is a popular choice for upholstery. Make sure you treat it as a delicate: suede is prone to fading and is easily soiled. The sample colors here are: (from left to right) gold, brown, lichen, and azure.

10. Leather: tough, long-lasting, and versatile, leather can bring real character to your upholstery. Leather is available in a variety of different finishes and colors, but it is often difficult to get your hands on large quantities, and you will find it expensive.

11. Silk blend: Silk is best for upholstery when it is cotton-backed, like these examples, which are 64 percent cotton, 36 percent silk. Be warned: silk is highly flammable.

12. Wool blend: These wool swatches are blended with linen (76 percent wool, 24 percent linen), making the wool base easier to clean, and introducing a soft feel to the material.

Textiles 29

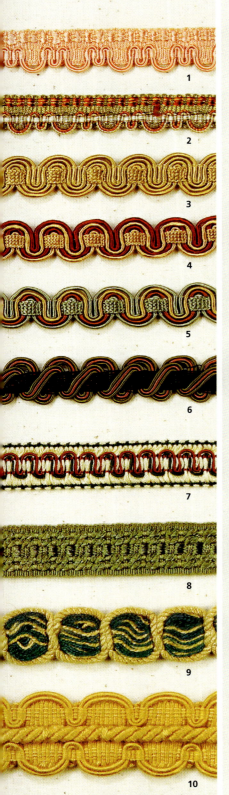

Trimmings

Trimmings include gimps, braids, and decorative cords that come in many different forms varying in color, size, and price. Both functional and decorative, trimmings can be used to add a bold accent, cover or disguise a stitched or tacked edge, enhance a frame's shape, lend an extra dimension to the furniture, or simply as a form of traditional decoration.

Trimmings are used on a chair or settee to cover the raw edges and tacks on the top cover, and also to protect the fabric from fraying. They also give the chair a finishing touch, and can be attached with glue, gimp pins, or stitching, depending on whether they are covering a line of tacks and a raw edge of fabric, or whether they are sitting on top of the fabric and hiding a stitched seam. Using a hot glue gun is normally preferable, but care should be taken to keep the glue away from both the fabric and your fingers.

Trimming types

1–2: This type of braid has a flat edge one side and a scalloped edge on the other, and is often more expensive than a scroll gimp or flat braid. This braid can be used either way depending on the finish required.

3–5: Inexpensive gimp with a scroll edge on both sides. The multicoloring of the gimp means different effects can be achieved, depending on which way the gimp is applied.

6: Scroll gimp with a wavy edge on both sides. This type of gimp has a loose weave which makes it good for chairs with curves and corners.

7–8: Inexpensive decorative braids that aren't good for curves or corners.

9–10, 16: Alternative braids in varying widths and colors. These are not as commonly used as the scroll gimps shown above.

11–15: A range of decorative cords in various colors and widths. Cords can be hand-stitched onto fabric either to hide a seam or for decorative effect.

17–18: Two types of decorative cord with flange. Cords such as this are sewed into the seams, usually on cushions. Use a welting foot to apply these cords, and keep stitching very close to the cord.

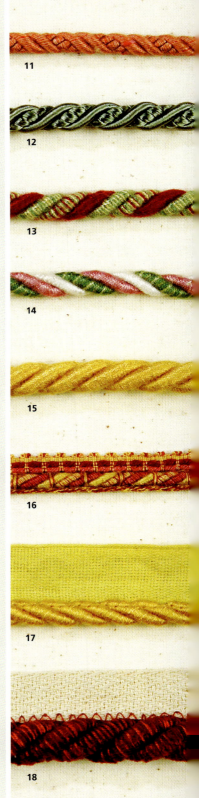

A lime green trim is used to spike this raspberry colored sofa, picking up the colors in the lampshade and cushions.

Techniques

What will distinguish your finished piece will be the shape and condition of the original item, the chosen textile—and how that suits the furniture and the interior in which the furniture is to be placed—and the skill and craftmanship that you have used in your reupholstery work. This section walks you through the techniques that you need to master.

Tools and materials

- **Ripping chisel:** To be used in conjunction with a mallet for levering out tacks and staples

- **Wooden mallet:** For striking a chisel, tack, or staple remover

- **Tack remover:** To lever out prominent tacks

- **Staple remover:** To remove staples

- **Pincers:** To remove tacks and staples

- **Scissors**

- **Tape measure**

- **Notebook** and **pencil:** For taking notes as you complete the upholstering process

- **Trash bags**

- **Camera:** For taking photos of the chair as it's stripped

- **PVA (craft) wood glue**

- **Upholstery apron:** Use an apron with pockets on the front to hold your tools, such as a tape measure and scissors

- **No. 2 wire wool**

- **Batting pad**

- **Cleaner** or **methylated spirits**

- **Tourniquet** or **cramp**

- **Wood adhesive**

- **Face mask**

Stripping

Before a piece of furniture can be upholstered, it needs to be stripped of its old coverings. Prepare to be surprised; once materials and stuffings are exposed you can estimate the age of the piece. At this point, make a list of the replacement materials you'll need so the real business of upholstering can begin.

Late Victorian or early Edwardian armchair
The chair is upholstered in cotton velvet with coordinating figured velvet on the front of the back and seat. Decorative fringing has been sewn along the bottom edge to cover the legs.

The piece of furniture you upholster may be a simple stool or chair, or it may be a large settee with cushions. Whatever the piece, the order for stripping remains the same—it's the upholstering process in reverse. So start with the covering underneath and work inward.

Preparing a chair for stripping

First, you must decide what sort of surface you will work on to strip your chair. Saw horses with a fixed wooden tray on the top are ideal, but make sure they are at a comfortable working height. Stripping can be a very dirty task, so wear an apron to protect your clothes from inevitable dust.

It's good working practice to have a camera and notebook at hand to take photographs and notes as you strip the chair. These will be useful to look back on and remind you what the piece looked like before stripping began, what stuffings were used, and how they were applied.

When stripping, take care not to damage the surface wood that shows (show wood), with the sharp tools. Take note of the state of the frame and check if any of the joints are wobbly.

If wobbly, the joints can be knocked apart with a mallet and re-glued. If the wood is rotten or damaged then you will need to find a furniture restorer to repair the damage. If dirty, the show wood may be cleaned using either denatured alcohol or a proprietary cleaner. The cleaning may be carried out at this stage, but the polishing is best left until immediately before attaching the final cover to prevent the polished finish from damage during the upholstering. (See pages 39 for cleaners and wood polishers.)

Upholstery materials

During the stripping process, make a note of the upholstering materials used as they are a good indication of what you'll need to replace them. The types of stuffing used will depend on the age of the chair, and should be replicated as closely as possible. Antique and old chairs usually have traditional stuffings, using some or all of the following: cotton or wool batting, hair, coir, black fiber, coil springs, burlap, and webbing; all of which are attached to the piece of furniture using tacks.

Sometimes, it will be clear that the piece has been reupholstered or re-covered previously. Look out for signs of this, as the work may not have been of the best quality and the materials used not ideal. Old stuffings are usually very dirty and dusty and should be discarded, as the dust could work its way through the top or bottom cover.

Keeping a record

Take photos and notes of every stage of stripping your chair. It is equally important to take pictures of the pieces of fabric that have been used, and make a note of exactly where they came from on the chair. The abbreviations listed here can be used to indicate the approximate size and location of each piece of fabric.

Fabric abbreviations

Location of components	Abbreviations of fabric components
B Bottom	A Arm
C Center	B Back
F Front	C Cushion
I Inside	S Seat
O Outside	F Facing
R Right	FF Front facing
L Left	W Wing
T Top	

For example, when a piece of fabric is removed from the right arm, it could be noted as "RA." The location always goes first. Make sure you apply the abbreviations as if you and the piece of furniture were facing each other, front on.

Stripping an armchair

Starting with the bottom cover of burlap, remove all the upholstery using a mallet and ripping chisel.

Continue to remove the upholstery until the sprung edge of the back and the springs on the arm are exposed.

What can be reused?

Material, stuffings, and springs should be reused only if they are clean and in good condition. This all depends on the age of the chair, the amount of use it has had, and where it has been stored.

It's not advisable to reuse tacks as they are often bent and have damaged tips, making it difficult to hammer them into the wood. Chairs that have a sprung edge on the front rail are attached to a cane; this should be retained if it's not damaged.

Reusing hair

You can wash and reuse hair as long as it has not broken up into small pieces. Clean it by hand in a bowl, or put it in the washing machine in a pillowcase carefully tied up with string. Then spread out the hair on an old sheet or towel and place flat to dry, either outside on a sunny day or inside in a warm place. Do not tumble dry—the hair will form tight balls that are difficult to tease out.

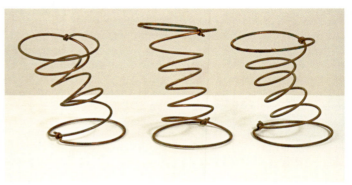

Modern chairs
Modern chairs (shown above and below left) are usually upholstered with foam, rubberized hair, and polyester batting, which are attached to the frame with staples.

Out of shape springs
Discard coil springs like these out-of-shape examples (above). The springs should go up and down vertically and not bend over to one side. Similarly, discard tension springs that have lost their elasticity and become overstretched, or serpentine springs that have become unaligned.

✻ **Upholsterer's Tip**
Protective gear
When stripping an old piece of furniture, wear a mask to avoid inhaling the dust.

REMOVING TACKS
Hold the chisel in your left hand and the wooden mallet in your right (reverse if you are left handed). Knock the edge of the chisel under the tack to remove it. Do not use a hammer because it will damage the chisel handle. When the edge of the chisel is under the tack's head, gradually lever the tack out of the wood. Old, rusty tacks sometimes break off, in which case it may be necessary to hammer home the remaining part of the tack to prevent further damage to the wood. Always knock the chisel in the direction of the straight grain of the wood to prevent the wood splitting.

Lashing the springs down

The springs must be lashed down to create a sprung unit. Failure to do so will result in a lumpy seat that goes out of shape very quickly. Follow the steps below to lash the springs down.

> ✳ **Upholsterer's Tip**
> As you lash the springs down, repeat to yourself: "Over the spring and underneath, over the string and through the loop."

1 Insert ⅝ in. (16 mm) tacks at a 45-degree angle into the frame on the back, front, and side rails, making sure they're aligned with the center of the springs.

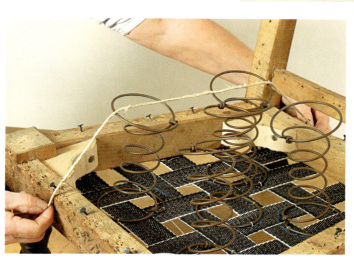

2 Measure a piece of laid cord one-and-a-half times the distance from the back to the front, or, if the springs are large, then twice the distance.

3 Now tie a slip knot in one end. Hook the slip knot over the tack at the back and hammer down securely.

4 Depress the spring at the back to the required finished height. Now place the cord over the spring and hold onto the top with your left hand.

5 Place the cord over and under the spring, taking the cord over the cord being held by your finger, and bring it forward through the loop to the right and pull tight.

6 Bring the cord onto the front of the spring, hold it securely with your left finger and thumb, then keeping a loop around your hand repeat the knot.

7 The distance between each spring on the top should be identical to the distance at the bottom. Repeat the knots at the back and front of each spring until you reach the front spring. With your left hand and arm, depress the springs to the required height and twist the cord around the tack at the front, tensioning it over the front rail to prevent the tack from coming out. Then hammer this tack home to anchor the cord.

8 Look at the position of the springs: they should be slightly tilted down to the sides of the chair but move up and down vertically when pressed. If they aren't in this position, the springs will become misshapen when the chair is used and make for an uncomfortable and distorted-looking seat.

9 Make a half hitch knot to secure the cord (see page 49).

Springing 53

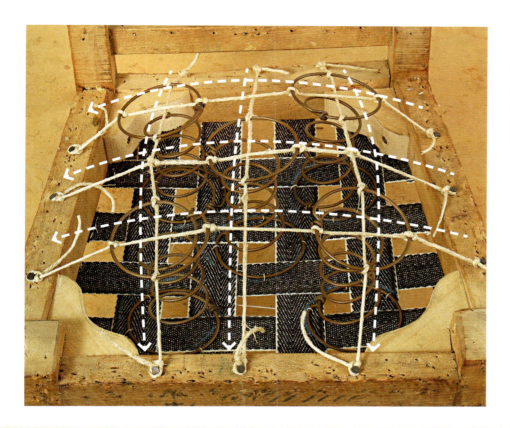

10 Repeat this process from the back to the front on each row of springs and then across it from side to side. Again, springs should be slightly tilted to the outside rather than the inside. Hammer home the tacks that secure the cord.

Other sized springs

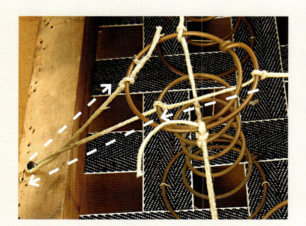

For springs 6 in. (15 cm) or over, it may be necessary to make a second knot on the last spring. Make the knot in the middle part of the spring, and then take the twine around the tack on the front rail, and return to the top of the spring with a knot. This will prevent the spring from becoming distorted.

If springs are over 7 in. (17.5 cm), then two rows of tying-down are required—the first one going through the middle of the springs, and the second row over the top. This helps greatly in the second tying-down and prevents the middle of the spring from going out of shape.

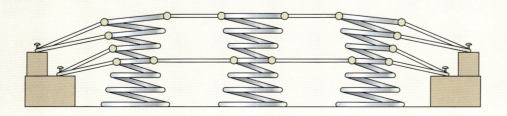

Tools and materials

- **Springs:** Use four for a chair, more for a sofa. Buy springs about 2 in. (5 cm) shorter than the main springs and a No. 10 gauge.

- **Webbing:** To attach springs to chair frame

- **Laid cord:** To lash springs down

- **Twine:** To attach cane to springs

- ⅝ in. (16 mm) and ½ in. (13 mm) tacks

- Clout nails

- Hammer

- Scissors

- Marker pen

Working a sprung edge

On large armchairs and settees with fully sprung seats, a sprung edge is necessary to make a firm edge to the seat. The springs should be approximately 2 in. (50 mm) shorter than the main springs.

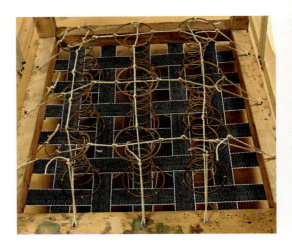

Creating a sprung edge

Place four or more springs on the front rail, anchor and tie them down, and attach to a piece of cane edge wire. Follow the steps below.

1 Place your springs on the front edge, positioning them between the rows of main springs, with one spring at either end of the rail. Use a marker pen to mark each spring's position.

2 Anchor the springs down with a piece of webbing threaded through the bottom of the spring. Tack each spring down on either of its sides, or anchor it with large staples onto the top of the front rail.

Working a sprung edge 55

3 Measure a piece of laid cord to go over the spring from back to front, one and a half times, and attach it with a tack on the inside of the front rail. Depress each spring to the same height as the seat springs already in place—approximately level with the bottom of the arm—and tie a knot as before on the top of the spring (see page 52).

4 Make another knot on the top front edge of the spring and bring the cord through the spring. Anchor on the front of the rail with a large tack.

5 Take a piece of edging cane or stout wire of the width of the seat and hold it to the center spring. Cut a length of twine of 1 yd (90 cm). Attach the cane to the spring as in the picture and pull the twine tight.

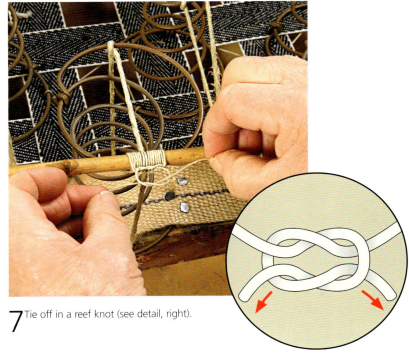

6 Blanket stitch the top of each spring to the cane, one end of the twine going to the right and the other to the left.

7 Tie off in a reef knot (see detail, right).

8 In order to bring the springs forward a little, attach short pieces of webbing folded in half over the middle coil, and anchor down with tacks on the front of the seat rail in a "V" position. Use two or three ½ in. (13 mm) tacks.

9 With a length of cord twice the width of the seat, make a tie from left to right going through the springs. Go up through the springs to the top in the middle, and then down to the other side. Anchor the tie at either end with a tack, and tie a piece of laid cord horizontally through the springs. Anchor with a tack.

10 Now that all the springs are anchored down securely, they are ready to be covered with burlap.

Other types of springs

Tension springs are attached to the top of the side rails of a chair by a standard metal plate with holes in it, or a fabric strip with eyelet holes.

Metal plates
Replace the metal plates if they are rusty and the holes worn. New plates can be obtained from an upholstery supplier and are easily attached with clout nails. Examine the fabric side fixings too, and if they show signs of wear or are rotten, replace them.

Attaching tension springs
The tension springs on a seat are attached to the side rails with a clip or staples. The seats of chairs are attached to the side rails. Different types of attachment are shown below.

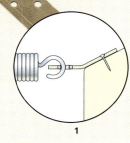 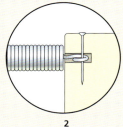 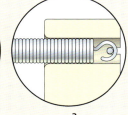
1 2 3

1. The tension spring is hooked into the appropriate hole in the metal plate.
2. The spring hook is placed in the slot and fixed with a vertical nail.
3. The spring is placed on the hook inside the chair rail.

Spring pads
If the original springs are old or overstretched, they should be replaced. Ensure the new springs are 1 in. (2.5 cm) shorter than the distance between the fixings so they are tight when stretched. To use them on a seat, cover them with a spring quilt or pad, and then a deep cushion. The spring pad is made from a piece of polyester batting sandwiched between two layers of decking with a pocket at either end for the spring to be threaded through. This way, the cushion won't get worn by the springs.

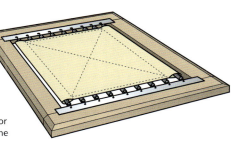

Serpentine springs
Examine the clips that anchor serpentine springs and make sure they're not damaged. If the springs are overstretched, replace them. The springs are linked together with wire or twine, which should be intact. Replace the ties if worn or missing so the springs don't move side to side.

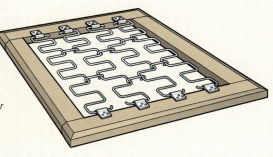

Tension springs
When tension springs are used on the back of a chair, they should be covered with a piece of burlap. This is to protect the subsequent stuffing from wearing under the movement of the springs. Subsequently, the burlap should be cut large enough to allow for a pleat to be made down the center: this will account for any movement created by the springs.

Tools and materials

- **Burlap:** To form a base for the stuffings
- **Tacks:** ½ in. (13 mm) improved and ⅝ in. (16 mm)
- **Scissors**
- **Magnetic hammer**
- **Tack remover**
- **Hammer**
- **Tape measure**
- **Staple gun** and **staples**
- **Springing** or **5 in. (12.5 cm) curved needle**
- **Length of twine**
- **Webbing**
- **Laid cord**
- **Batting**, **hair**, **coir**, **foam**, or **paper foam**
- **Foam tack roll**

Staple gun

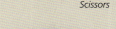
Scissors

Preparing a burlap base

Burlap is a cloth used in upholstery as a platform to cover webbing and springs. It supports the stuffings that are later applied. This section explains how to apply burlap—first to seats without springs, and then to seats with springs.

Burlap is a stout cloth that comes in two qualities. The cheaper one has a loose weave, while the more expensive one is stronger with a tighter weave. The latter is preferable, because the closeness of the weave prevents hair and some dust from passing through it, and it's also more hard wearing.

※ **UPHOLSTERER'S TIP**
When applying any fabric to a piece of furniture, ensure the grain of the fabric goes straight from the back of the chair to the front, and from side to side (as shown, right).

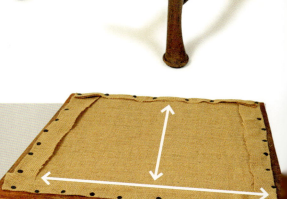

Applying the burlap to drop-in seats

Once the webbing is complete on the top of the frame, it needs to be covered with burlap so that the stuffings don't fall out of the chair.

1 Measure the seat top from the back to the front, and from side to side. Cut a square piece of burlap, allowing an extra 1 in. (2.5 cm) around the square for turnings. Center the fabric on the top of the back rail, and fold over 1 in. (2.5 cm) along the raw edge.

2 Temporarily tack through the fold onto the top of the back rail using ½ in. (13 mm) tacks. Apply three or four tacks about 2 in. (5 cm) apart. Take care when tacking, and if the wood shows any signs of splitting, use a smaller and finer tack or a staple from a staple gun.

3 Repeat the tacking on the top of the front and side rails, but this time without folding the fabric over. Tack through the single layer of burlap and then repeat this on the side rails. Make sure the burlap is stretched over the webbing tightly and that the weave of the fabric is straight (both vertically and horizontally) when the chair is viewed from the front.

> ✳ **UPHOLSTERER'S TIP**
> *Always initially anchor the fabric in the center of the four sides.*

※ **Upholsterer's Tip**
When attaching fabric, always work from the center of the rail to the corners—never go around in a circle or you are likely to end up with a bunch of fabric in the last corner, and the weave of the fabric is unlikely to be straight.

4 When the burlap has been temporarily tacked all around the fabric and is taut, hammer the tacks home.

5 Fold the excess burlap over on the three remaining sides and tack down. Then neatly fold the corners on top of the frame.

6 Trim the excess fabric with scissors to neaten the burlap. This cut should be approximately 1–2 in. (2.5–5 cm) from the tacks. The seat will now have a firm base and is ready for stuffing.

Preparing a burlap base   61

Stuffed over-seats with or without coil springs

Stuffed over-seats without springs have burlap covering the webbing, while seats with springs, such as the one below, have the springs covered with burlap. When measuring these seats allow extra burlap for covering the springs.

1 Set the burlap on top of the springs. Take care when tacking down that hollows do not form in the burlap between the springs: the burlap should just sit tightly on top.

2 Fold the burlap at the back and anchor with three temporary tacks. Using an upholsterer's hammer with a curved head is helpful here if the bottom rail of the chair's back is in your way.

3 With the burlap unfolded on the top, place three tacks at the front.

4 Place three tacks at either side to ensure that the grain of the burlap runs straight from front to back and from side to side.

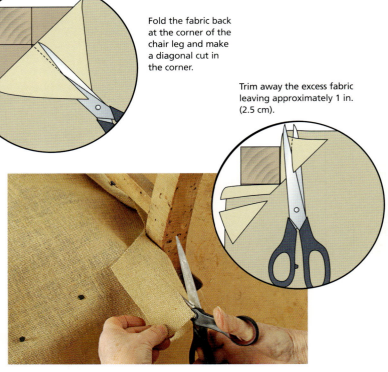

Fold the fabric back at the corner of the chair leg and make a diagonal cut in the corner.

Trim away the excess fabric leaving approximately 1 in. (2.5 cm).

5 Having inserted several tacks on each side, the burlap must be cut to go round the back corners. At each corner, fold the material back and make a mark on the inside corner. Then make a cut diagonally across to this mark

6 Take the burlap either side of the back leg and fold back the excess. Trim this off leaving 1 in. (2.5 cm) turning.

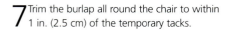

7 Trim the burlap all round the chair to within 1 in. (2.5 cm) of the temporary tacks.

8 Add extra tacks where necessary about 2 in. (5 cm) apart. When all the tacks are in place and the burlap sits tightly on top of the springs, hammer the tacks home.

9 Finally, fold the excess fabric over and tack down permanently.

Preparing a burlap base 63

Attaching the burlap to the springs

The burlap is stitched to the springs to stabilize its position and to ensure that all the subsequent stuffings are attached to the springs. Sew the burlap to the springs using a springing—or 5 in. (12.5 cm)—curved needle and a length of twine.

1 Take the curved needle and thread from the top of the burlap, under the spring, and up through the burlap. Tie a slip knot on the top (see page 49).

2 Again, take the needle and thread through the burlap, under the spring, and back through the burlap, about a third of the way around the spring. Make a knot on the top.

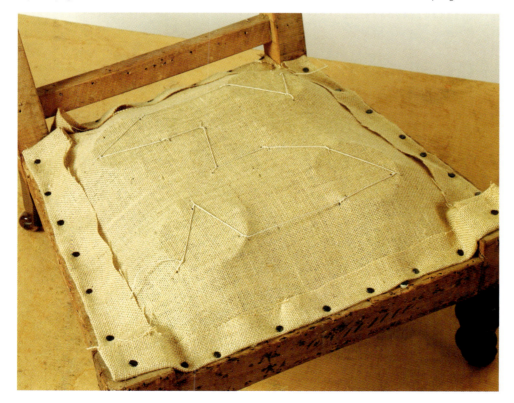

3 Repeat the process another third of the way around. Move to the next spring without tying off the twine. Repeat this process until all springs have been tied in. If the twine runs out, attach another length using a reef knot (see page 55).

Chairs with a sprung edge on front rail

The burlap on a seat with a sprung edge, such as the one below, covers the main springs and forms a well between the main springs and those on the front edge. When filled with hair, this well separates the main springs from the front sprung edge.

1 Tack the burlap with temporary tacks on the back, front, and side rails, leaving the excess piece of burlap at the front. This will eventually go into the well behind the front edge springs. Sew the burlap to the main springs using three knots per spring.

2 At the back corners, fold the burlap back and make a cut into the corner. Trim away excess (see page 62).

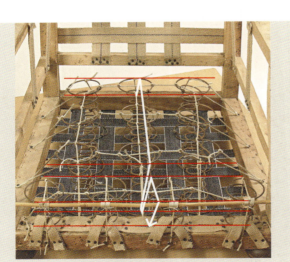

CALCULATING BURLAP FOR FRONT RAIL SPRUNG EDGE
To calculate the size of the burlap needed when there is a sprung edge on the front of a chair frame: measure from the top of the back rail over the springs, down into the well formed by the sprung edge, over this edge and onto the front rail. Measure the widest distance from side to side, and add 1 in. (2.5 cm) all around for turnings.

3 Release the tacks at the front, and tuck the burlap down into the well between the edge springs and the main springs.

Preparing a burlap base 65

4 Place a piece of string or webbing in the well that is formed, and anchor at either side on the top of the side rail with large tacks. This is known as a well cord. If placed correctly, the cord will sit in the well, tacked at either side on the top of the side rail.

5 Fold the burlap back to reveal the main springs and cut several pieces of cord to act as guy ropes over the well cord. Using a curved needle, take these pieces of twine through the burlap and around the well cord, allowing at least one guy rope between each spring.

6 Secure the end with a slip knot and pull up tight.

7 When all the guy ropes are in place, tack the end of the cord onto the top of the front rail using ⅝ in. (16 mm) tacks or staples.

8. Bring the burlap over the sprung edge and tack onto the front of the rail. At the corners, make a neat pleat (as shown, below).

9. Sew the springs on the front edge to the burlap using a blanket stitch and secure the side pleats similarly.

Using burlap elsewhere

Burlap can also be used as a platform for the stuffings on the arms, wings, and backs of chairs. Apply it using the same method that has been described for the seats.

Always temporarily tack initially— follow the principle of tacking first on the back, then the front, on the top and bottom, and then side to side. When the burlap is tight, the temporary tacks can be hammered home. Where webbing is used because there is no rail, cut the burlap with a diagonal cut, taking it through the gap between the webbing and the back rail, and then stitch it to the webbing using a running stitch.

Burlap is tacked onto the side rail, and then stitched to a strip of webbing.

The finished effect should look neat and feel durable.

Forming an edge roll

An edge roll, found on the edge of certain types of chairs, replaces a stitched edge and prevents hair being pushed to the back of the seat when it is used. There may be an edge roll at the front, or on the sides as well. On a stool, the edge roll may go the whole way around. An edge roll may also appear around the scroll edge of an arm, or wing, in which case it replaces a stitched edge. An edge roll was often used in Edwardian times to save using expensive hair.

MAKING AN EDGE ROLL
An edge roll can be made with batting, hair, or coir and formed into a roll with burlap. Cut the burlap an extra 4 in. (10 cm) larger than the size of the chair where the roll is to go, and tack onto the front rail. Roll pieces of white cotton batting or handfuls of hair into the excess burlap, and roll up tightly, inserting tacks in the back of the roll, making sure the roll is flush with the front rail. Edge roll can also be bought in foam or paper form, which can then be attached using large tacks, and is used principally around the scroll end of arms and wings.

1 Cut the burlap several inches (or centimeters) longer than is necessary and place a wad of white cotton batting (or another relevant stuffing) on the top at the edge of the chair.

2 Roll the burlap over the batting and tuck it underneath to form a tight roll.

3 Insert long tacks at the back of the roll to anchor it down. Fold the corners over the stuffing and tack down neatly.

Use foam tack roll to create a scroll edge around the arm of the chair. This can also be used around a wing, or sometimes on the edge of a seat.

Tools and materials

- **Hair:** For the stuffing
- **Coir, black fiber, or batting:** For the stuffing
- **Scrim:** To cover the hair
- **Springing needle or large curved needle:** For stitching bridle stitches
- **Long double-pointed needle:** For stitching stuffing ties
- **Twine:** For stitching
- **Scissors**
- **Improved tacks ½ in. (13 mm) and ⅜ in. (10 mm)**
- **Hammer**
- **Regulator**
- **Rasp:** To create a beveled edge on the front rail
- **Tape measure**
- **Tailor's chalk**

※ Upholsterer's Tip
Always use twine from the center of the ball to prevent it from unwinding.

Twine

First stuffings

Now that the piece of furniture has a secure base, it's time to think about the stuffing. On a traditional piece, this will be of hair, coir, or black fiber, or maybe rubberized hair.

Nursing chair
This nursing chair will have a sprung stuffed over-seat with a stitched edge.

Most chairs have stuffing of some sort. The age and type of chair determines the kind of stuffing used and how much is required. If it's a traditional chair, it may have one or two layers of hair stuffing, followed by a layer of batting, depending on the chair and whether or not it has springs. When hair is used, it's attached to the chair by bridles, which are loops of twine stitched into the burlap.

The amount and thickness of stuffing required is determined by the size of the chair and the finished height. If the chair requires a modern stuffing, then foam or rubberized hair can be used. The latter can sometimes also be used effectively on traditional pieces.

The stuffing on traditional chairs varies according to the type and shape of the piece. Some chairs have only one stuffing, for example a drop-in seat, while others, such as a stuffed over-seat, require at least two stuffings and a stitched edge.

The following section describes how to do the first stuffing on drop-in seats and stuffed over-seats.

Drop-in seat (traditional style)

Drop-in seats only have one layer of stuffing and no stitched edge; as a result, it's best to use real animal hair. They don't need a stitched edge as the frame of the chair supports the stuffed pad (see opposite).

Pincushion seat

A pincushion seat has a single stuffing of hair on top of the burlap and webbing.

When the pad is made of hair, bridles must be stitched onto the burlap (see opposite). Hair can then be stuffed under the bridles to form an even mat, covered with white cotton batting, and finally, covered with muslin.

Sewing bridles

Bridles are loops that are sewn into the burlap to hold the hair in place. Without them, the hair would be piled in an uncontrollable heap on top of the chair. Follow the following steps to make the bridles.

1 Cut a 10 ft. (3 m) length of twine, thread the springing needle, and anchor the twine in the back left-hand corner of the burlap.

2 Make a slip knot (see page 49) and pull tightly to the burlap.

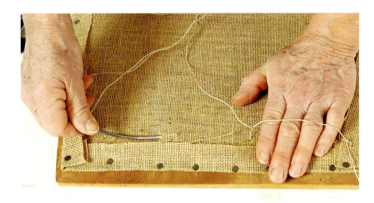

3 Sew four to five overlapping loops across the back of the chair. The loops should be as wide as the palm of your hand and be loose enough for your hand to fit underneath easily. The loops should not be knotted down individually, but left to loosen or tighten according to the hair underneath.

4 The loops can be sewn in rows or in a square shape, as in the picture. The rows should be no more than 3 in. (7.5 cm) apart. The twine is finished with a reef knot (see page 55).

Inserting stuffing

Stuff approximately 1 lb. (250 gm) of real hair under the bridles evenly over the seat, making a slight dome shape in the middle. Then tease the hair out to form an even mat without holes.

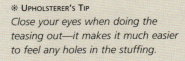
❋ Upholsterer's Tip
Close your eyes when doing the teasing out—it makes it much easier to feel any holes in the stuffing.

1 Insert a handful of hair under the first loop that was made, and then do the same under the second loop and subsequent loops. Make sure that the hair reaches the edge of the seat frame.

2 If the loops are filled in the order they were inserted, then each one tightens up the next one and helps to make the bed of hair even.

3 Continue stuffing the seat until all the loops are filled with hair, and then tease the hair together to make a nice flat mat. If there are any holes in the mat, more hair should be added.

Covering with batting

Cover the hair on the seat with a layer of white cotton batting to prevent the hair from working its way through the covering of muslin and final top cover. Cut the white cotton batting to size, place it on top of the hair, and then tear it so that it fits around the edge of the chair.

1 First, measure the area to be covered with batting to determine how much is required.

2 Batting is difficult to cut with scissors and is better torn. Torn edges are also easier to tease together if a join has to be made. Remove the paper backing from the batting and place it on top of the hair. Then tear the surplus away so that it just covers the hair but does not hang over the wooden frame at the side, as this may prevent the chair seat from fitting the frame.

Covering with muslin

Cover the white cotton batting with a piece of muslin. This should be big enough to completely cover the stuffing and be tacked underneath the frame. The muslin is then tightened over the stuffing, relieving the tension from the final top cover.

1 To measure for muslin, take a tape measure over the top of the batting and underneath the frame, adding 2 in. (5 cm) extra so that the muslin can be held easily in the hand when tensioning.

2 Place the muslin on the top of the batting, making sure that it's on squarely with the grain going straight from back to front and side to side.

- frame
- webbing
- burlap
- hair
- batting
- muslin

❋ **UPHOLSTERER'S TIP**
If you don't have a tape measure on hand, use your forearm as a guide. The distance from the tip of your finger to your elbow measures about 18 in. (45 cm), which is the approximate depth of an average chair.

3 Turn the whole seat over and position the seat and stuffing centrally on the muslin.

4 Before tacking down, make sure that the stuffing of hair and white cotton batting does not overhang the sides of the frame. You should tuck the stuffing in or remove it if there is too much.

5 Pull the muslin firmly over the hair and batting and insert a temporary tack on the underneath of the frame.

6 Insert several more temporary tacks on either side of the original tack, then turn the frame around and do the same on the other three sides.

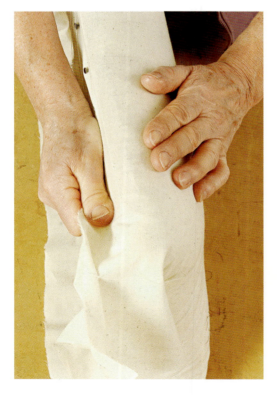

7 Removing two or three tacks at a time, tighten the muslin using one hand to smooth the muslin to the back and the other to retack.

8 When retacking, make sure the stuffing on top of the frame edge is even and with no dips. If there are dips, more hair or batting should be added underneath the muslin.

First stuffings

Anchoring and cutting the corners

Once the muslin has been tightened at the sides, you will need to neatly tack down the corners. The pleats formed on the corners should be as flat as possible.

1 Take the muslin over one of the back corners of the seat and secure with a tack underneath.

2 Draw a "V" shape either side of the tack to indicate where the cut should be made.

3 Cut up to the "V" shape in a straight line, and then along the line of the "V" making a "Y"-shaped cut.

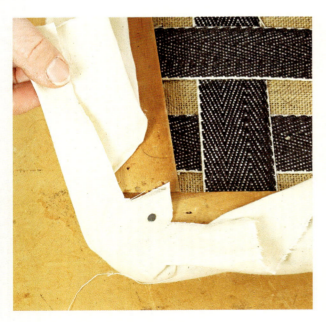

4 Cut away excess fabric after the "Y" cut has been made to reduce the amount of fabric that will needed to be folded under. Make folds in the muslin at the corners, and cut away any excess fabric that is underneath the fold, before tacking it down.

5 Neaten the pleats with the blunt end of a regulator.

6 Tack one pleat down with a small tack. Trim away the fabric beyond the tack and then tack the second pleat, trimming away any excess fabric. Repeat this on all corners.

7 Check that the muslin is still tight on the top. Now that it is tacked all around and the corners are finished, the tacks can be hammered home (as seen, left).

Chairs with a stitched edge

Black fiber and coir are better stuffings than real hair for chairs with a stitched edge, as they eventually form a firmer pad and edge roll. However, they must be used generously.

> ✻ **UPHOLSTERER'S TIP**
> When you are measuring fabric for the seat, remember to add at least 2½ in. (6 cm) all around for tucking under.

Because it is softer, hair is often more difficult to form into the firm edge required later on for a stitched edge, but you can use it. Remember that hair from an old chair can be washed and reused (see page 36). The seat illustrated here is a frame that sits on top of a chair frame anchored with a peg at the front (see also page 81).

You will need about 1 lb. (250 gm) of stuffing (hair, coir, or black fiber) for a dining seat averaging 18 in. (46 cm) by 17 in. (43 cm). You may have to add more later if necessary. Follow the first stuffing instructions as for the drop-in seat (see page 69–70) for stitching bridles and stuffing with hair. Then follow the instructions below before you stitch the edge.

1 Stitch bridles onto the chair top as previously described (see page 69) and stuff with at least 1lb. (250 gm) of hair, coir, or black fiber. The hair should be teased into an even mat over the whole surface with no dips or holes.

2 Typically, a piece of scrim measuring around 24 in. (61 cm) square is about right for an average dining chair. Lay the scrim over the stuffing.

3 Temporarily tack the scrim down on the outside of the underside of the rails at the back and front, and on both sides.

4 Ensure that the weave of the fabric is straight in both vertical and horizontal directions. Failure to do so will cause later problems.

Stuffing ties

Stuffing ties are stitched through the scrim to the burlap and are used to anchor the scrim in place. Where there are springs, take the stitches through the burlap only and not through the springs and webbing.

1 Using tailor's chalk, draw a square on the scrim about 4 in. (10 cm) in from the perimeter of the seat.

2 Take the unthreaded point of the needle right through the scrim and the burlap at the back left-hand corner of the drawn square. Return the needle up through the scrim 1 in. (2.5 cm) away.

4 Pass the needle through the scrim once again following the chalk line. Make each stitch length approximately 1 in. (2.5 cm).

3 Having pulled the needle completely through the scrim, make a slip knot on top, and tighten.

5 When all the stitches are complete, pull the twine tight and tie with a bow. This allows for adjustment later.

You should continue your stitching all around the marked square, as shown above.

76 Techniques

Tacking down the scrim

Now the scrim is stitched in place with stuffing ties, it needs to be tacked to the beveled edge of the frame.

❋ **Upholsterer's Tip**
It is difficult to tack into a corner, so bevel the edge with a rasp.

1 Remove the tacks from underneath the chair frame and add extra hair to the stuffing to ensure that the rolled edge is filled generously, but evenly.

2 Tuck the scrim underneath the hair to form a round edge that is full of hair. (The scrim can be trimmed at this stage if there is too much to tuck under.)

3 Tension the scrim to form a firm edge before tacking it down.

4 Tack the scrim onto the edge using ⅜ in. (10 mm) tacks. Start in the center of the chair frame and move outwards.

5 Keep adding tacks along the front edge, putting the tacks in temporarily, and working to within 2 in. (5 cm) of the corners. Repeat this process on the back and sides, trimming the scrim if there's too much to tuck under.

First stuffings

Front and back corners

Once you have tacked the scrim around the chair, it's time to finish the corners. Make a neat square pleat at the front. The type of pleat you make at the back depends on the type of chair you're using and the corner's finish.

Front corners

1 Tack to the end of the side rail. Bring a side piece of scrim around the corner to the front and make a small cut 1 in. (2.5 cm) from the corner.

2 Unfold the fabric, and cut a square of fabric using the cut already made as a guide.

3 You may find you have to add more hair under the scrim on the corner. It is much easier to pleat the fabric around hair than air!

4 Tack the scrim to the edge at the front corner. Now take the fabric round to the side ready to make a pleat.

5 Make a front-facing pleat with the excess fabric. Ensure that the pleat lies on the straight weave.

6 Trim away the excess fabric, tuck underneath, and tack down onto the chair rail.

7 Using the blunt end of a regulator, neatly tuck the scrim underneath the hair, making sure there are no wisps of hair showing.

8 Before tacking the edge, use the regulator to make sure the hair underneath the scrim is evenly distributed.

9 Secure the pleat of the scrim by putting a tack in the corner. Also, anchor the side of the pleat with a tack and hammer home.

Unusual back corners

1 Some seat frames have the corner cut out and will need to be treated in a different way. Start at the back corners and begin by folding the scrim back.

2 Make sure there is plenty of hair in the corner for the scrim to go around and if more hair is needed, pack it in well using your thumb.

3 Make a diagonal cut in the scrim just up to the cut out corner.

First stuffings

4 Fold the fabric underneath, and place a tack in the corner of the top of the frame.

5 Having cut away any excess scrim, use the blunt end of the regulator to help tuck the fabric underneath into a neat pleat.

6 Repeat this on the other side of the corner using the regulator to neaten the fold.

7 After tucking down on both sides of the corner, tack down neatly on the top of the rail.

Checking tension

Once the seat has been temporarily tacked all around, check the tension of the scrim. If the tension is even, hammer home the tacks. The stuffed seat should have a firm, vertical rounded edge—not too tight, nor too loose.

Now that the tacks are all hammered home, use a regulator to move the hair underneath the scrim, as shown above and right. This ensures that the pad is neat and even. The seat is now ready for the edge roll to be stitched (see over the page).

Stitching an edge

A stitched edge is formed by one or more rows of blind stitching followed by an edge roll. Blind stitching is so called because the stitches are visible from the side of the chair but not the top.

Regulator

Tools and materials

- **A double-pointed needle:** Use an 8 in. (20 cm) or 10 in. (25 cm) depending on the size of the seat.
- **Regulator:** To regulate the hair.
- **Good quality twine:** Barbour No. 3 or No. 4.
- **Scissors**
- **Glove**
- **Highlighter**
- **Tailor's chalk**

Double-pointed needles

Highlighter

Tailor's chalk

The aim of this technique is to build up a firm edge on a chair that will keep its shape when sat on. It can also be applied to arms, wings, and the top of backs of chairs—in fact any place where a firm edge is required.

It is usual for two rows of stitching to be applied to a dining chair, but an armchair or large sofa with a deep seat will require three or four rows.

The aim is to create a firm edge of hair so that when the seat has been used for some time, the stuffing remains in place and does not go out of shape. You should end up with a solid edge roll, straight side and square corners, as seen here.

※ **Upholsterer's Tip**
When using twine, to ensure that you pull it as tight as possible, wear a glove to prevent the twine from cutting into your palm.

Starting to blind stitch

The process starts with a slip knot. First, thread your needle with about 10 ft. (3 m) of twine. Always use this amount as 6½ ft. (2 m) will never be enough and 13 ft. (4 m) will fray before you reach the end. If you are right-handed, then work from left to right. Reverse this if left-handed.

Take care when taking the needle and thread through the burlap—do not take it through the springs, if there are any. Similarly, don't take the needle and twine right out of the scrim to form a stitch on the top, as this will impede the tightening of the hair. The twine should go around the hair between the burlap and scrim and pull toward the edge—if you can visualize this, it becomes more obvious why a stitched edge is necessary.

1 With the left hand side of the chair facing you, take the unthreaded end of the needle and insert it into the scrim close to the back corner. Scrape the edge of the rail as you do so.

2 Pull the needle through the scrim, and bring it out near to the stuffing ties so that the eye of the needle can be seen.

Bring the needle through the scrim so that the eye can be seen.

3 Return the needle back through the scrim, about 1 in. (2.5 cm) from the chair leg.

4 Once you have pulled the needle and twine through, place the needle in a safe place on top of the chair with the sharp point facing away from you, and tie the twine with a slip knot (see page 49).

First row of blind stitching

Blind stitches can be seen from the side of the chair, but not from the top. A different chair is used here.

1 Keep the twine from the slip knot on the left, and insert the unthreaded end of the needle into the scrim about 2 in. (5 cm) along to the right. Pull the needle out close to the stuffing ties in the center of the chair, but only until you can see the eye and no further.

2 Return the needle back through the scrim to where the slip knot is making a wide "V" shape underneath the scrim, brushing the frame of the wood as the needle is brought through.

> ✴ **Upholsterer's Tip**
> *Always use Coats Barbour twine, usually No. 3 or No. 4, and never cheap twine which is weak and flawed. Nylon twine isn't suitable either because it's not a natural yarn and has a tendency to slip when stitched.*

3 Wind the left twine around the needle three times, and pull the needle through. As a safety measure, put the needle in the top of the chair, pointing away from the body.

4 Taking care not to break the twine, pull the knot that has formed toward you tightly to the right, so that the knot slides along.

If the stitch has been made correctly, with the twine from the left being wound round the needle three times, the knot will slide along (as seen here) as opposed to remaining in a tight knot.

Stitching an edge 83

5 This stitch should not be in a tight knot, but travel along. Work the stitch around the chair, including the back if possible.

Take care at the corners so that they are not flattened but kept square (as seen, right). A short stitch on the corner is useful. Think about what the twine is doing under the scrim—it should be pulling the hair toward the edge in a fat wedge, not a thin one.

6 Once you have reached the end of a row make a short stitch and then wind the twine in your left hand around the needle, followed by the twine in your right hand. Pull the twine through to form a knot. Avoid taking the twine around the inside of a chair leg—it is always better to finish off at the end of a row and start again with a slip knot.

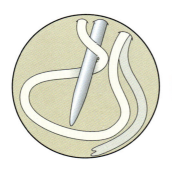  

Joining twine with a reef knot
Since a granny knot will come undone when pulled, join twine using a reef knot (see page 55). Make the knot close to where the twine has been pulled through on the chair. It's not possible to take the knot through the scrim when sewing.

Second row of blind stitching

On a stuffed over-seat, a second row of blind stitching is necessary to build up the stitched edge. In this row, the stitch is the same as in the first row, but the needle and twine emerge halfway between the stuffing ties and the chair edge. This moves the hair closer to the edge.

> ❋ Upholsterer's Tip
> If the chair has a deep seat and a deep layer of hair, then use several rows of blind stitching to build up the edge further.

1 Make a second row a ½ in. (13 mm) above the previous row. To stitch accurately, mark it on the scrim with a highlighter or tailor's chalk.

2 Start with a slip knot—as with the first row of stitching. Now, take the needle into the scrim on the marked line to emerge from the top of the scrim— about halfway between the edge of the chair and the stuffing ties.

3 The stitch should be repeated all round the chair as with the first row.

Edge Roll

Now that there's a firm amount of hair at the edge, it's ready for the final roll. Adjustments can be made with the regulator to ensure the even distribution of the hair along the edge, and to prevent it from being soft or lumpy.

1 Mark a line on the side of the scrim ¼ in. (6 mm) above the last row of blind stitching. Now make another line on the top of the scrim approximately 1 in. (2.5 cm) from the edge of the top surface, taking the inside corner of the back leg as a guide.

Stitching an edge 85

2 Starting with a slip knot, take the needle through the scrim and out completely on the top, then return through the fabric about 2 in. (5 cm) back. Pull through.

3 Wind the twine around the needle three times, and pull the needle through to complete the stitch. Aim to get as much hair as possible into the roll to make it firm.

4 Make sure the side of the stitched edge is vertical, and not sloping in or out. Beginners may find this procedure difficult, but practice will help you improve. When going around a scroll edge on an arm, one row will be enough. The stitching is now complete.

A regulator (right) is used to gather the hairs at the edge of the chair so that the roll is full.

Some variations

For chairs that have some show wood around the area where the roll needs to be, for example, on the inside back of a chair, use a large curved-needle instead of the double-pointed straight one. Then only one row of blind stitching is usually needed, plus the edge roll.

When stitching an edge around the scroll end of an arm or wing, it's usual to have only one row of blind stitching followed by the roll edge (as seen, right).

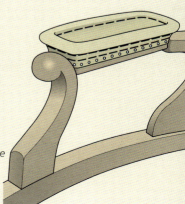

Second stuffings

Tools and materials

- **Twine:** for bridles
- **Hair:** Approx 1 lb (250 gm) per small chair
- **White cotton batting or cotton batting:** to cover the hair
- **Muslin:** to cover the batting
- **Curved needle**
- **Magnetic hammer**
- **⅜ in. (10 mm) fine tacks**
- **Scissors**
- **Tape measure**
- **Pencil for marking**

Curved needle

✻ **Upholsterer's Tip**
The upholstery process is identical for both sofas and chairs: a sofa just needs larger pieces of fabric and more stuffing. The order of upholstering a large chair is normally: back, arms, wings, and finally, the seat.

Now you have finished the first stuffing and stitched edge, your chair will have taken on a new shape. Gone is the nice rounded finish and in its place is a rather uncomfortable looking seat, with a firm edge and a hollow middle. A second stuffing is required to make the chair comfortable again.

The hair that once covered the chair has been pulled to the side, and now the second stuffing will fill this space to recreate the rounded shape that was previously there. Once the second stuffing of hair has been positioned, cover with thick cotton batting, and then muslin. The white cotton batting prevents the hairs creeping through the muslin and top fabric, which would be uncomfortable to sit on. The use of muslin enables the stuffing to be tightened before the top fabric is put on. This also means that if the top fabric ever needs to be replaced, then the stuffing will stay in place. Follow the steps below to make this second stuffing.

Attaching bridles

With the stitched edge completed, more bridles need to be stitched to the scrim. Follow the instructions for these as you did in the first stuffing (see page 68). Bridles stitched on a larger piece should be 4 in. (10 cm) in length and in rows that are 4 in. (10 cm) apart. The stitches should reach the extremity of the seat, both in width and length. Backs and arms require the same process. Using a curved springing needle and twine make loops on the scrim to anchor the hair.

Second stuffings 87

Stuffing hair

Stuff the bridles with real hair, or washed old hair—as long as the hair hasn't disintegrated into small pieces.

✷ Upholsterer's Tip
*Useful measurements:
The length of your forearm, from fingertip to elbow, is approximately 18 in. (45 cm) The length from your thumb to your first joint is approximately 1 in. (2.5 cm) The span of your palm, from little finger to thumb is approximately 8 in. (20 cm).*

1 Take handfuls of the hair and tuck it under the bridles, starting at the back and following the bridles in the order that they were stitched in. When this has been done all over the seat, back, or arm, tease the hair out so that it forms a thick mat with no dents or holes.

2 Where the hair has gone thin under the scrim with the first stuffing, make sure the area is well covered with the second stuffing. The whole stuffing should be 2 to 3 in. (5 to 7.6 cm) deep, depending on the size of the chair. If you are reusing hair, make sure that it's well teased out and not in tight knots.

Covering with white cotton batting

The next step is to cover the hair with white cotton batting, which comes in two thicknesses. The thinner batting—which is a two-and-a-half ounce weight (28 gm)—is usually thick enough. This prevents the hair working its way through the muslin and top fabric. Measure from the back of the seat to the front, and tear off a piece of white cotton batting the same size—it's better torn, as it is difficult to cut with scissors.

1 Remove the paper or backing from the batting and place on top of the hair.

2 Tear the white cotton batting so it hangs just over the side of the chair roll. If the roll isn't exactly vertical, place a piece of batting along the side edge to recreate a straight edge.

Anchoring muslin

Use muslin to cover the white cotton batting and anchor down all the stuffings.

> ❋ **Upholsterer's Tip**
> When tacking, ensure that the grain of the muslin runs straight across in both directions.

1 Measure the length of the seat from the bottom of the back rail, over the stuffing, down to the bottom of the front rail, and across the middle to the sides. Allow an extra 2 in. (5 cm) of material to tack down. Tack the muslin with temporary tacks to be tightened later.

2 Place the muslin on top of the batting and anchor first at the front, then at the back with temporary tacks into the single thickness of fabric. The muslin does not need to be turned under.

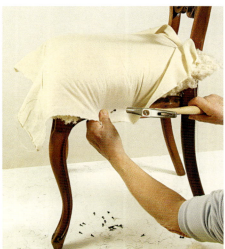

3 Continue this temporary tacking at the side edges of the chair, gradually working from the center to the corners.

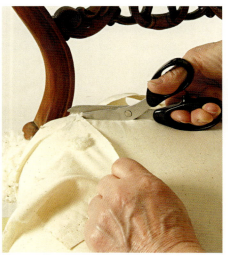

4 Make cuts at the back corner, by folding the muslin back into a "V" shape and cutting into the corner, as with the burlap and scrim.

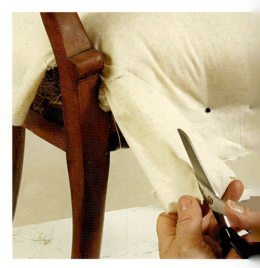

5 The ears of fabric produced by the first cut can then be removed leaving 1 in. (2.5 cm) to tuck under.

Pleating

It's now time to pleat the front corners. This can be done as a straight pleat when the top of the leg of the chair is square shaped or with two pleats making a tulip shape when the chair leg has a curved or shaped corner.

1 Tack the muslin to the end of the side rails, bring it to the front, and pull it down slightly. Tack the muslin onto the front rail, just around the corner, and make a fold in the material.

2 Cut away any excess that's in the fold, which generally takes the form of a square shape. A cut edge always sits better than a fold.

3 Tuck in the excess fabric and make a pleat in the muslin, using the straight grain of the fabric on the edge of the pleat. Use the blunt end of the regulator to make the pleat sit straight. This pleat can then be tacked down.

Tulip pleat

A tulip pleat is best suited to a chair with curved corners. It has a double pleat which will hug the edge of the show wood neatly.

1 Pull muslin over the front corner of the chair leg and anchor with a tack.

2 A pleat should be made either side of the center tack, using the blunt end of the regulator to neaten the pleat. Both of these pleats can then be tacked down. (See page 95 for a finished tulip pleat.)

> ✲ **UPHOLSTERER'S TIP**
> *Muslin that has been treated with a fire retardant is often brittle, so be careful that it doesn't tear at the cut corners. Often, using untreated muslin and a fire retardant barrier cloth is a better idea.*

Tightening muslin

The muslin needs to be taut. To achieve this, either sit on the chair, or put a weighty object on it for 24 hours. Then, smooth the top of the muslin with your left hand, pull it down with the right, and tack down with temporary tacks on the side of the rails before permanently tacking.

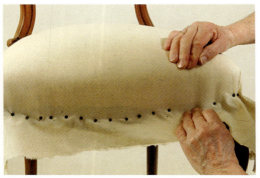

1 Remove the temporary tacks one at a time and retack after tightening down as shown in Step 2. If any holes in the hair can be seen through the muslin then the muslin will have to be removed and more hair added under the batting.

2 After removing the temporary tacks, tighten the muslin using your hand to smooth the fabric from the top to the sides.

3 Once you are satisfied that the seat is firm and nicely rounded, hammer the tacks home and trim the muslin close to the tack line. Make sure the line of tacks is not too close to the show wood, if there is any, because the muslin will be seen when the top cover is attached.

Applying muslin to the seat of large armchairs

Marking and cutting the back corners of the muslin on large chairs is often difficult. You will need to push the muslin through from the front, and tack it down at the back.

1 Measure the gap between the inside back legs. In this example it is approximately 20 in. (51 cm).

2 Measure from the inside corner to the bottom of the back rail. In this example it is 5 in. (12.5 cm).

3 Measure the chair at the widest point—from back to front and left to right. Cut a piece of muslin, adding 3 in. (7.5 cm) all round for the turnings. With the muslin folded in half lengthways make a mark 10 in. (25 cm) from the fold and 5 in. (12.5 cm) from the raw edge. Cut diagonally toward this mark to form a wedge shape. Push this shape through from the front of the seat to the back and tack down on the outside of the back seat rail.

Attaching new coverings 95

2 Attach the center of the fabric with three tacks at the front, back, and sides so that the weave of the fabric is straight on the chair from back to front and side to side.

3 Fold the fabric at the corners back and cut to the inside corner.

When you pull the fabric down into the corner of the leg of the chair it should sit tight and neat (as seen above).

4 Open up the cut and pull the fabric to either side of the leg.

5 Fold the excess fabric back and cut off the ears at the side and the back.

6 Fold the excess fabric underneath. Check that the fold is on the straight grain of the fabric and tack down. If the fold is on the bias, it won't sit straight. Repeat on the other back corner.

7 This chair has a rounded edge at the front corners so a double or tulip pleat is required. Take the fabric over the corner and tack down.

8 The pleats should meet at the edge of the show wood. Use the blunt end of the regulator for perfecting the crease of the pleat and make sure that the gimp or braid (see pages 112–113) will cover both the tacks and the raw edge when it is applied.

The straight back rail

In this sequence you will learn how to attach fabric to chairs with straight rails, sloping side rails, square front legs, and straight back legs. You must make a "Y" cut in the fabric to go round straight rails and insert a small piece of fabric in the gap created at the side.

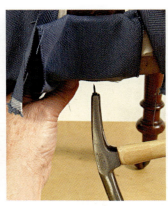

1 Mark the fabric as for the muslin on page 75 and make a "Y" cut to take the fabric round the rail. Choose a small piece of fabric 2 in. (5 cm) longer and 3 in. (7.5 cm) wider than the gap, making sure that the pattern and direction of the pile go in the same direction as the fabric at the back of the seat. Take a strip of back tacking or narrow card the width of the back rail and tack through the card and fabric.

2 Pull the fabric down over the gap and tack underneath the seat frame.

3 Fold the seat fabric over the raw edges of the insert and tack underneath. Any fullness at the back of the chair is taken up with one or two pleats.

The sloping side rail

It's awkward to make the cut on a side rail and easy to cut in the wrong place so take care and work slowly.

1 Fold the fabric back and mark the rear cutting point with a pin. Note that this mark will be further forward than you expect.

2 Create a second mark with a pin and make a "Y" cut to these marks. Never cut right up to the mark; further cutting can be done if necessary but a cut cannot be rejoined.

If the fabric has a small amount of stretch and the cut has been made correctly, then you will be able to pull the fabric round and fold it over without inserting an extra fabric piece (as seen above).

Square front legs

Square front legs with show wood on the corner require several cuts and a straight pleat to make a neat corner.

1 Fold the fabric back and make a diagonal cut to the corner of the leg. Trim off excess.

2 Make a similar cut at the top of the leg. Trim off the excess, leaving enough to fold under and around the top of the leg. Use a regulator for this.

3 Take the folded fabric around the corner, pulling it down slightly. Anchor with a tack. Make a diagonal cut in the fold underneath.

4 Cut out the excess fabric underneath the fold. Cut out a square shape and make another diagonal cut into the top corner of the show wood.

5 Fold the fabric underneath, form a neat pleat on the corner, and tack home. This can be anchored permanently with either a tack, gimp pin, or decorative nail.

Straight back legs

Pull the top fabric down, mark either side of the chair leg, and cut.

1 Pull the fabric down to the leg. Mark either side of the leg and make a "Y" cut to the marks.

2 Fold the fabric on either side of the leg, making pleats where necessary. Tack underneath, and hammer the tacks home. Only those at the front, above the show wood, will need to be covered with gimp or braid.

Tools and materials

- Hair
- Finishing fabric
- **Muslin:** to cover the hair
- White cotton batting
- **Polyester batting** (medium weight): to protect the white cotton batting
- **10 in. (25 cm) double pointed needle**
- Nylon twine
- **Scraps of muslin/webbing or burlap:** to act as butterflies behind the knots
- Regulator
- **Skewers:** to indicate button marks
- Pins
- Covered buttons
- Tape measure
- Ruler

Hair

✻ UPHOLSTERER'S TIP
Professional upholsterers have buttoning machines to make secure, covered buttons. Kits for making buttons can be bought at fabric shops, but the buttons often come apart when they are tied down.

Deep buttoning

Deep buttoning on upholstery was introduced in the nineteenth century to add opulence— although not necessarily comfort—to seats. It is widely seen on the backs and arms, rather than seats, of traditionally upholstered chairs and requires the skill of an experienced upholsterer. Deep buttoning is also found on modern chairs and headboards where the use of foam makes it a much easier task.

The stuffing underneath the deep buttoning was traditionally a firm pad of hair, which has been replaced in modern chairs with foam and rubberized hair. It is important to set out and mark the positions of the buttons carefully. Make sure you mark up the fabric accurately so the pleats formed between the buttons lie flat and are of a uniform size. Usually, the buttoning has a diamond pattern where the length is greater than the width. Different shaped patterns should be left until you have mastered the diamond shape. The following instructions are for real hair.

1 Decide on your buttoning pattern and mark the burlap base accordingly using skewers. The type of pattern you use will depend on the size of the space available for buttoning and the style of the chair. As a guide, a diamond shape 5 in. (12.5 cm) wide by 7 in. (17.5 cm) long is a good size to work from, but it can be smaller or larger. For comfort, and a pleasing appearance, place the bottom row of buttons slightly above the lumber area, and in line with the top of the arm. Once the position has been decided, replace the skewer mark with a chalk or pen mark on the back and front of the burlap.

Deep buttoning   99

Chair back measurement

4.5 in. (11.5 cm) | 5 in. (12.5 cm) | 5 in. (12.5 cm) | 4.5 in. (11.5 cm)

4.5 in. (11.5 cm)
7 in. (17.5 cm)
10 in. (25.5 cm)

Muslin measurement

6 in. (15 cm) | 6.5 in. (16 cm) | 6.5 in. (16 cm) | 6 in. (15 cm)

6 in. (15 cm)
8.5 in. (21.5cm)
11.5 in. (29.5 cm)

2 in. seam allowance

2 Cut a piece of muslin large enough to completely cover the buttoned area. Allow an extra 1½ in. (3.75 cm) between all the buttons, and from the buttons to the edge. Also allow for a 2 in. (5 cm) seam allowance all around. On a chair back, the extra muslin goes between the bottom rails and is attached on the outside of this rail. Draw center lines on the straight grain of the muslin to establish the center of the fabric. Then mark up the muslin, allowing an extra 1½ in. (3.75 cm) between the button marks. For example, a diamond shape five inches (12.5 cm) by seven inches (17.5 cm) will become six and a half inches (16.25 cm), by 8½ in. (21.25 cm). Make sure the markings on the muslin are on the straight grain of the fabric, and that enough fabric is left at the top and bottom to be tacked down at the edges.

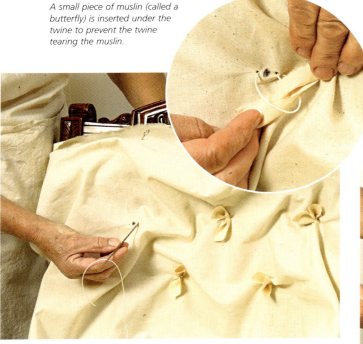

A small piece of muslin (called a butterfly) is inserted under the twine to prevent the twine tearing the muslin.

Place a butterfly of burlap or webbing under the slip knot at the back of the chair before pulling it tight.

3 Thread a double-pointed needle with nylon twine. Line up a button mark on the muslin with a mark on the burlap. Take the threaded end of the needle through the muslin and burlap, about ½ in. (1.25 cm) to one side of the mark. Unthread the needle at the back leaving one of the ends of the twine at the back of the burlap. Repeat this with the end of the twine at the front, but ½ in. (1.25 cm) from the mark in the opposite direction so that the twine is through the muslin and burlap either side of the mark. Place a butterfly under the twine at the front to prevent the twine tearing the muslin.

4 Tie a slip knot at the back of the burlap, place a butterfly under the knot and pull it tight. Repeat this with two horizontal rows of button marks. Pockets should now be forming in the muslin.

5 Stuff the pockets with plenty of hair. Real hair is softer and easier to use for this than coir or black fiber. This stuffing should be even, with the resulting pleats sitting on top of the hair rather than in a hollow. Large quantities of hair are needed to fill the pockets evenly. Add more hair by pushing it underneath the hair that is already there, rather than over the top. This makes a better shape around the button. The muslin can be anchored temporarily at the edges with skewers.

6 A regulator may be used to move the hair into awkward corners and to perfect the pleats. Repeat this process with all the other buttons until the stuffing between the buttons is complete. Secure the slip knots at the back with a reef knot.

✻ **Upholsterer's Tip**
The pleats should always face downward on the back of a chair and forward on a seat.

7 Now you will fix the muslin. Make sure the grain of the fabric is straight, and then make vertical and horizontal pleats from the button nearest to the frame edge. Secure with a skewer. You may have to add more hair to give a round finish to this edge. Smooth the fabric so that there is no fullness or gathering fabric between these pleats. Incorporate any surplus fabric into the pleats.

Deep buttoning 101

8 When the buttons are tied down correctly and the stuffing is even and taut, then fix it permanently with tacks; or stitch it to the scrim. Stitching is often easier—use a slip stitch and nylon thread.

✳ Upholsterer's Tip
When using patterned material think about where the pattern should lie—it can be in the center or positioned randomly. Buttons can be made into different sizes, although the most common size is ½ in. (13 mm).

9 Cover the whole area with white cotton batting and then polyester batting. Make large holes in both layers, to indicate where the buttons will sit. The polyester can form a tight ring on the top cover if the holes are not large enough. The chair is now ready for the top cover.

10 Cut a piece of fabric the same size as the muslin. If it has a pattern then position it to be in the correct place on the chair when it is buttoned. Mark the button positions on the fabric with pins, making the same allowance for the buttons as on the muslin. Do not use chalk or a marker pen here, as the mark will show if you need to alter the button's position. Thread the double-pointed needle with 18 in. (45.5 cm) nylon twine, and take the twine from the front through the top fabric, to the left of the pin.

11 Remove the pin from the button mark and take the needle through the hole in the polyester, white cotton batting, and muslin to the back of the burlap, going to one side of the butterfly. Remove the twine from the needle leaving an end at the back of the burlap. At the front, thread the other end of the twine through the button. Now rethread the needle and take it through the fabric and stuffing to the back of the chair, passing the other side of the butterfly.

12 Make a slip knot and pull tight as you did previously with the muslin. Ensure that the button is sitting flat in the hole. When repeating this with the other buttons, test the position of the mark by placing your finger on it, pushing it into the hole, and then marking it with a skewer. Ensure the fabric between the buttons is taut and on the straight grain. Repeat this process on the arm. If there are no holes in the frame for the button twine to be taken through then pull it through on either side of the frame and anchor with a tack.

If a neat pleat forms diagonally between the buttons, then tie in the second button. Repeat this on the next button to form a diamond pattern (as seen, right). If the fabric has been marked correctly on the straight grain then the pleats will lie flat. When tightening the buttons, make sure the pleats are all folding down, this prevents dust gathering in them.

13 After tightening the buttons at the back, trim the batting at the front so it will be clear of the tacking down of the top fabric. Now, temporarily tack the top fabric to the frame using ⅜ in. (10 mm) tacks. Tack the spaces between the pleats first and then form the remaining fabric into a pleat.

A staple gun with a nozzle (as seen on the left) instead of a flat bed, is ideal for anchoring the top fabric.

Vandyking

Tools required

- Fabric
- Nylon twine
- Marking pen
- Ruler
- Scissors

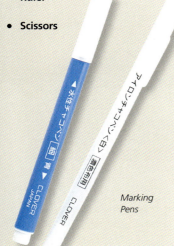

Marking Pens

In the context of upholstery, vandyking means to join two pieces of fabric in deep buttoning, without the need for a straight seam. It is most often found on large pieces such as Chesterfields and headboards.

Mark the position of the buttons carefully and accurately on the fabric (see page 98–102) and draw diagonal lines between each button, while keeping the pattern and direction of the pile of the fabric in mind.

1 Draw an extra cutting line ½ in. (12 mm) from the edge of the line of buttons to be joined on both pieces of fabric and cut away the excess in a zigzag line.

2 When the excess has been cut away in a zigzag line on both pieces to be joined, they should mirror each other as shown.

3 Pin or baste these two pieces together and machine stitch along the drawn line making sure that the button marks are together.

4 Cut nicks into the seam so that it will stretch over the padding when the buttons are inserted.

5 This simple method of joining will result in an invisible seam when deep buttoned. Here it is viewed from underneath.

Shallow buttoning

Tools and materials for shallow buttoning

- **Buttons**: use a button covering service or a buttoning machine as for deep buttoning.
- **Double-pointed needle**
- **Nylon twine**
- **Scraps of burlap for butterflies**
- **Skewers**
- **Pins**

Double-pointed needles

Shallow buttons sit on the surface of the top fabric rather than in a deep cut hole. They are used for decoration and for taking up slack material on chairs with curved backs.

Shallow buttoning on a chair takes place after the top fabric has been applied and before the outside cover has been attached. Shallow buttons are often used on modern chairs to anchor two pieces of fabric together. They're also applied to the tops and bottoms of cushions to help stabilize them. String is tied underneath the buttons with a reef knot.

Applying shallow buttons to a cushion

Shallow buttons are used on the back and front of this cushion. For the back of a chair, wind twine around a piece of fabric called a "butterfly" and tie securely.

1 Mark the positions of the buttons with pins or skewers on the top and bottom of the fabric. They can be arranged in a square, as shown below, or in a variety of other symmetrical patterns.

2 Pass the threaded end of the needle through the pin mark on the cushion.

※ **Upholsterer's Tip**
Do not secure the buttons until you have decided on the placement of all of them. This ensures that the tension is the same on all of the buttons.

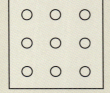 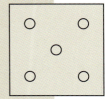 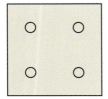

These three layouts (above) show alternative button positioning. The button patterns are flexible according to individual requirements.

3 Now, take the needle further, through the mark on the back of the cushion, but only until the eye of the needle can be seen.

✻ UPHOLSTERER'S TIP

Place the shank of the button in the hole. This prevents it from wobbling on top of the fabric.

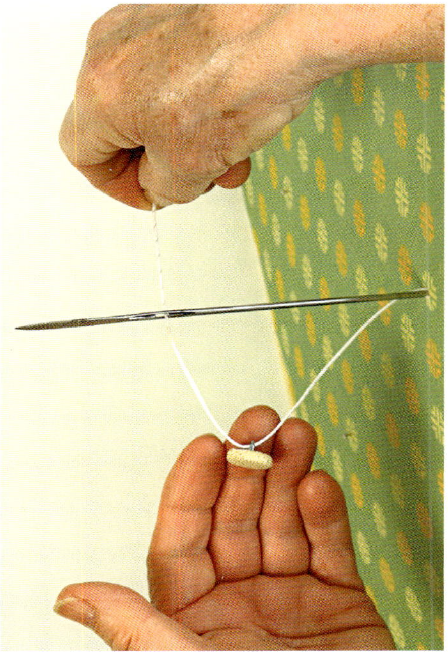

4 With the needle still in the cushion, remove one end of the twine from the needle. Pass this end of the twine through the button shank, rethread the needle, and pull the twine through to the back.

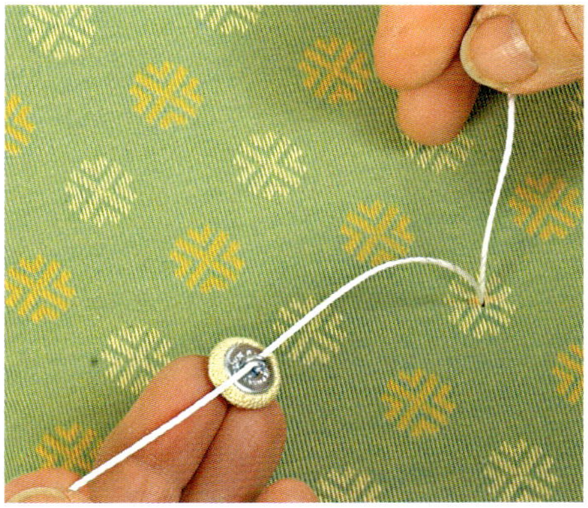

5 Unthread the needle and pull the threads so the shank of the button on the reverse side sits in the hole made by the twine.

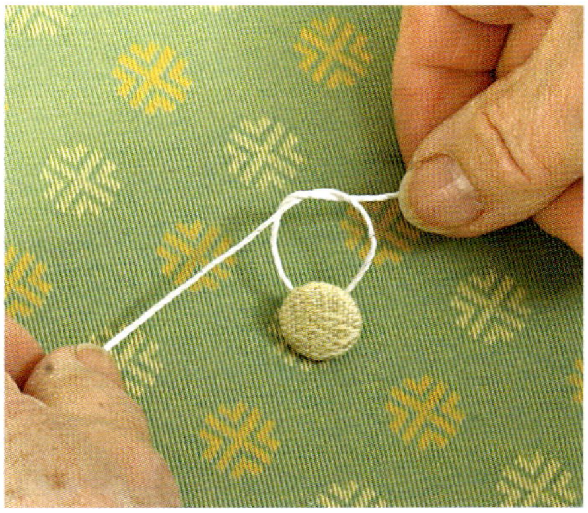

6 Tie the ends of the twine together with a reef knot and tighten.

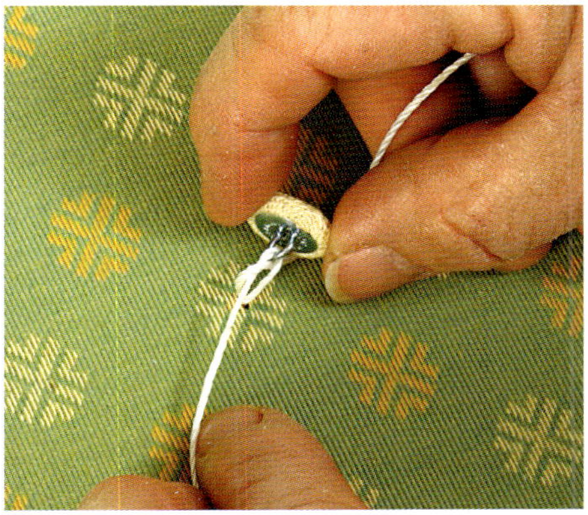

7 Secure the knot underneath the button.

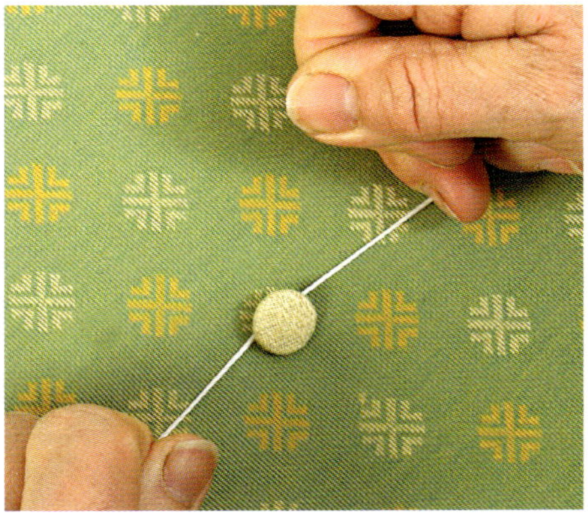

8 Pull the knot tight and add another one.

Tie shallow buttons that are seen only on one side of the chair or cushion, at the back. Knot the twine round a piece of fabric known as a butterfly to prevent the knot pulling through to the front (as seen, right).

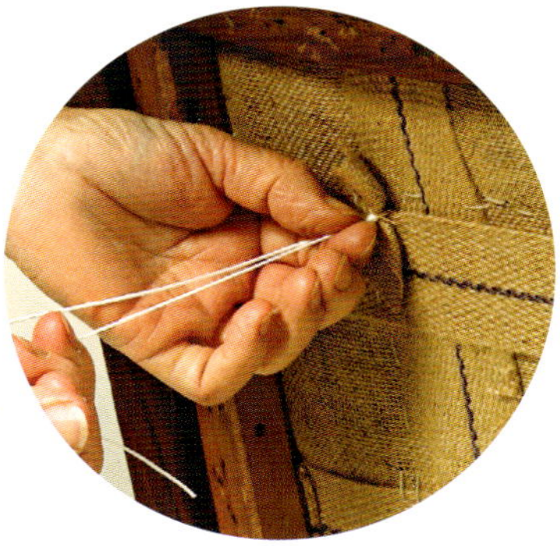

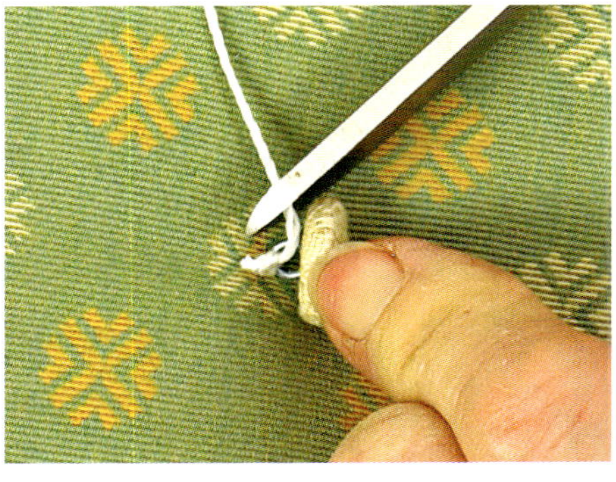

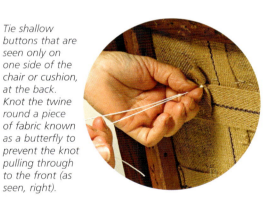

9 Cut the ends very short so that the button can sink into the hole.

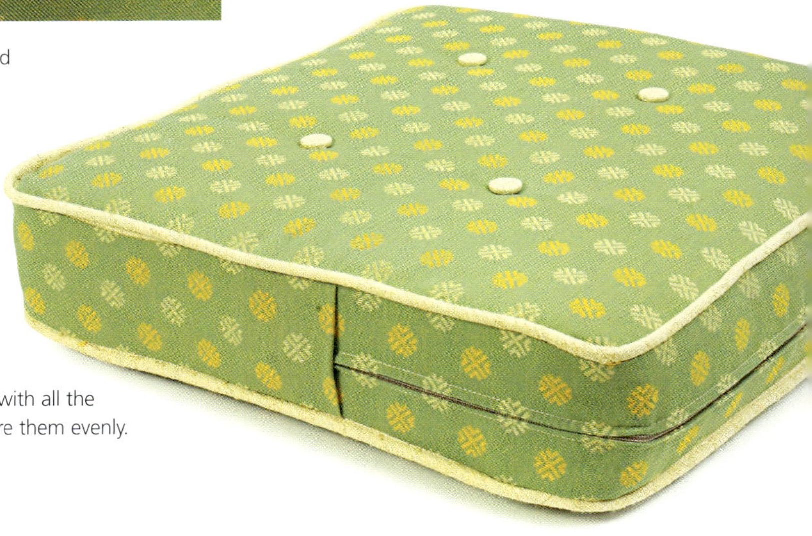

10 Repeat the steps with all the buttons and secure them evenly.

Tools and materials

- **Sewing machine** with a zipper foot and double-welt foot.
- **Ruler**
- **Pencil**
- **Rotary cutter or scissors**
- **Welt cord, single and/or double**

Rotary cutter

Making single and double welt

Single welt (piping) is used to decorate or disguise seams on upholstered chairs. It can be made of the same fabric used on the chair, or a contrasting one. Sew the welt onto the fabric or attach to the chair with tacks. Double welt is used only for decoration, replacing gimp or braid, and should sit next to the show wood where it doesn't protrude.

Welt is made from strips of fabric machine-sewn around a cord, using a welt or zipper foot. You will need to measure the chair for all of the welt that is required and then cut enough strips to stitch together to make up this length. Cut the strips of fabric to 2 in. (5 cm) wide on the bias (at 45 degrees) if the welt is to go around corners. Otherwise cut the fabric on the straight grain. Keep the type of fabric in mind when cutting on the cross or straight grain—for example, striped fabric always looks better when cut on the bias.

Single welt

1 Line up the ruler on the fabric so that 2 in. (5 cm) strips can be rotary cut at 45 degrees. Alternatively, mark the fabric with a ruler and pencil and cut along the line with scissors. Cut the ends of the pieces at identical angles so that they can be joined together.

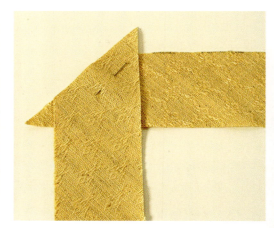

2 Place the first strip of fabric face down on the second strip of fabric and pin them together so that the edges overlap.

❋ Upholsterer's Tip
To make it easier to sew the small pieces together and to save thread, sew one piece after another and cut the threads when they are all joined.

Making single and double welt 107

3 Machine stitch all the strips together to make a piece long enough for the required length.

4 Place the welt cord on the wrong side of the fabric strip.

5 Fold the fabric strip over the welt cord, hold in place with a horizontal pin, and machine stitch very close to the cord, using a zipper foot.

BULKY SEAMS

With thicker fabric, make "V" cuts in the seam allowance to reduce the amount of fabric in the join. Then press the seams open with your fingers (left).

Carefully machine stitch over the join (right).

Double welt

For double welt, use an industrial machine and a double-welt foot. Cut the strips of fabric ½ in. (13 mm) wider than for single welt to allow for the extra cord.

1 Stitch a row of welt the same as for single welt using a single welt foot. Trim the one piece of fabric close to the stitched line.

2 Take a second piece of welt cord, place it beside the original row, and bring the fabric over the top.

3 Keeping the fabric taut over the cord, sew down the middle between the two rows. Use a double welt foot.

Tools and materials

- **Sewing machine**
- **Fabric**
- **Zipper:** measure back plus 6 in. (15 cm)
- **Tape measure**
- **Scissors**
- **Pins**
- **Welt:** made to match or contrast
- **Pencil**

Measuring tape

✻ Upholsterer's Tip

Make a mark or snip in the center of each side of the top and bottom fabric pieces to help match them up later.

Scissors

Making box cushions

Armchairs and settees sometimes have box cushions on the seat and the back to make them higher and more comfortable. These cushions have a lining filled with foam, feathers, polyester, or a mixture.

Your box cushion should fit neatly onto the seat of the chair with a welted edge on the top and bottom to stop the seams from wearing. Make the foam at least 4 in. (10 cm) deep for maximum comfort. Insert a zipper at the back of the cushion so the cover can be removed and washed. The zipper should go around the back corners and down the sides several inches to prevent the cushion from tearing when it is inserted. A pocket for the zipper will keep it out of sight. Take care when cutting the fabric for the top and bottom walls to ensure the pattern matches up evenly—especially when using striped fabric.

Measuring the cushion fabric

Two pieces of fabric should be cut for the cushion top and bottom. Allow an extra ½ in. (13 mm) seam allowance all round. Cut two pieces of fabric for the cushion wall, allowing the same seam allowance plus an extra 1 in. (2.5 cm) width in the section where the zipper is to be inserted. The length of the two wall pieces when joined should be 6–8 in. (15–20 cm) longer than the circumference of the cushion. The zipper should always be positioned at the back of the cushion.

Above: finished cushion with contrasting welt

Making the cover

Sew the welt to the top and bottom components of the cushion, lining up the raw edges. Then, sew the cushion wall first to the top and then to the bottom, ensuring that the corners line up with each other.

1 Take the top or bottom piece of fabric. Start at the middle of the back of the fabric and line up the raw edges of the fabric and the welt. Begin stitching about 3 in. (7.5 cm) from the end and machine stitch close to the line of stitching on the welt.

Making box cushions 109

Secure the fabric with the needle in the down position and pull the welt round to realign the raw edges (as seen left).

2 Stop sewing about 3 in. (7.5 cm) from the corner, and leave the machine needle in the down position. Make a diagonal cut in the welt from the corner of the main fabric to the stitched line of the welt.

3 Sew to this cut point, leaving the needle in the down position.

4 Turn the fabric and welt 90 degrees so that raw edges are lined up again. Continue stitching around the corner and then down the straight side of the cushion.

5 Repeat these four steps with the other three corners and stop stitching at least 6 in. (15 cm) from where you started. Cut the welt so that the two ends overlap by several inches.

Techniques

Joining the welt

Join the welt with a discreet diagonal seam.

1 Undo the machine stitching several inches at both ends of the cord.

2 Cut the ends of the fabric diagonally so that they overlap. Make sure that both diagonals go in the same direction and join them together with a pin.

3 Machine sew the join.

Cut a "V" shape out of either side of the seam to remove excess fabric and help the seam lie flat (as seen, right).

4 Lay the cord over the fabric join and cut between the two.

5 Fold the fabric over the cord, lay it flat on the cushion piece, and machine sew together. Take the other piece of fabric and repeat the steps to make the cover and join the welt.

Attaching a zipper end

Cushions come in varying sizes so it is best to buy zippers by the yard or meter, which can then be cut to size. A zipper end is required for each cut length.

1 Make diagonal cuts at the end of the zipper, leaving one end longer than the other.

2 Attach zipper end first on the long side and then on the shorter side.

3 Holding both ends in one hand gently pull zipper end down zipper.

Making box cushions 111

Inserting the zipper

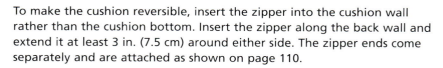

The wider piece of cushion (as seen, above) has been cut in two lengthwise to accommodate the zipper.

To make the cushion reversible, insert the zipper into the cushion wall rather than the cushion bottom. Insert the zipper along the back wall and extend it at least 3 in. (7.5 cm) around either side. The zipper ends come separately and are attached as shown on page 110.

1 Having cut the strip of fabric in two, attach the zipper to one side. Fold the fabric over, pin, and baste the zipper in place before machine stitching.

2 Now machine stitch the second piece of fabric to the zipper stitching in the same direction as strip 1. Hold the ends of the zipper together while stitching to ensure that they align correctly. Then join the two pieces of cushion wall together at both ends to make a circle, and attach to the cushion top.

Joining the wall to the top of the cushion

1 With the cushion wall on top, line up the raw edges of cushion top and wall, positioning the zipper part at the back of the cushion. Machine stitch these together starting several inches from the zipper end. Fold the excess fabric of the cushion wall into a pleat.

2 Machine stitch over this fold.

3 Repeat steps 1 and 2 on the cushion wall and bottom, making sure that the center marks and corners are lined up on the top and the bottom. Machine stitch with the wall on the top as before.

Tools and materials

- **Gimp or braid**
- **Gimp pins**
- **Decorative cord**
- **Slipping thread:** on which to sew cord.
- **Glue gun or fabric glue:** to attach the trimming.
- **Colored gimp pins:** to anchor the trimming at start and finish. Color to match top fabric.
- **Scissors**

✲ Upholsterer's Tip
If the gimp has hot glue on it, take care when pressing it down. You don't want to burn yourself.

Finishing the chair

Braid and gimp are used to cover raw edges of top fabric when it has been trimmed near to the show wood. The braid or gimp should complement the top fabric in color and texture. A decorative cord is used as a decorative trim or to disguise a join in the top fabric.

Gimp or braid is found on chairs with their show wood exposed. It can be glued or tacked into place using gimp pins, and occasionally it is sewn on by hand. Use decorative or trimming cord instead of welt on scroll edges to disguise a seam in the fabric. The most common type of trimming is a scroll gimp, which has a loop to go around curves and corners, unlike a straight braid. Before attaching the gimp, you will need to check that the trimming is wide enough to cover the tacks anchoring the top fabric and make adjustments accordingly. A trimming can also be made from a narrow tube of matching fabric anchored to the chair with decorative nails.

Attaching braid or gimp

Measure the chair for the length of trimming needed, and add a further 1 in. (2.5 cm) at either end for turnings. Heat the glue gun if using one. Where the trimming needs to be joined, butt the joints together in the center of the rail rather than joining at the corner.

1 Starting at the back corner, put a little glue on the right side of the trimming about 1 in. (2.5 cm) from the end.

2 Place this end face down on the chair, covering the raw edge of the fabric and the tacks or staples. Press down.

Finishing the chair 113

3 Insert a colored gimp pin in the end of the trimming and fold it back so that the right side is now on top.

4 Spread glue along 3–4 in. (7.5–10 cm) of trimming and press down. Repeat all along trimming to within 4 in. (10 cm) of the end.

5 To finish off, cut the trimming 1 in. (2.5 cm) longer than the required length. Fold it over and glue.

USING GIMP PINS

Gimp pins are available in several colors: use to finish a braid, or to anchor it firmly to a mitered corner.

MITERED CORNER

When the trimming has to go around a corner, it needs to be mitered. Insert a gimp pin in the corner and then fold braid or gimp over. Glue down.

Attaching underside barrier cloth

To finish the chair, you should attach a barrier cloth to its underside. This will neaten up all edges and act as an effective dust barrier. Chairs that have tacks inserted on the underside should be finished off with a close weave fabric, such as platform lining or a synthetic platform cloth. Burlap is sometimes used but it does not make an effective dust barrier because of its open weave. Chairs that have polished wood underneath should be left as they are.

Follow these steps to attach the barrier cloth:

1. Turn the chair upside down and use padded saw horses or a table to support the arms. Secure all the tacks.
2. Trim any excess fabric.
3. Cut a piece of black lining fabric large enough to cover the base of the chair, allowing an extra 1 in. (2.5 cm) all round for turnings.

4. Turn under the raw edges of the fabric and tack down, using ⅜ in. (10 mm) tacks at 2 in. (5 cm) intervals. Once again, start tacking in the center of the back and front of the rails, ensuring that the grain of the fabric is straight from back to front and from side to side.
5. At the corners of the legs, fold the fabric back, make a diagonal cut to the corner, and trim away any excess.

Techniques

Tools and materials

- Domed or decorative nails
- Nail strip and matching nails
- Tacks or gimp pins
- Hammer, preferably rubber-tipped
- Chalk

Hammer

Close nailing and adding a nail strip

Close nailing and nail strips cover the cut edges of leather or vinyl chairs. They come in a brass or antique-bronze finish and are used instead of a gimp or braid. Decorative nails can be bought in many colors and shapes and are used on the front of a leg—to anchor the fabric, for example.

Close nailing is time-consuming and an exacting task for the amateur upholsterer. The nails need to touch each other in an exact line. Only one has to be out of place to ruin the effect. Care also has to be taken with the wood as the tack's holes can damage the edge of the frame. Creating a gauge can make the task easier. A nail strip is a strip of faux nail heads butted up to each other with holes at intervals along the strip for a matching nail to be inserted. The strips come in yard lengths (or meter lengths) with different sized holes and different finishes, so make sure you use matching nails.

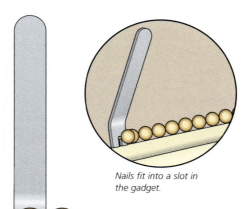

Nails fit into a slot in the gadget.

Side view of metal gadget

Front view of gadget

When close nailing, amateurs are advised to nail to a chalk line, and to make holes with a bradawl to mark the spot for each nail. The nails should be evenly spaced or touching. Gimp pins can be used instead of tacks to tack down the top fabric, as they have a small head. It is important for the domed heads of the nails to cover the line of tacks or staples. Metal hammers can damage the heads of the nails so use either a rubber hammer or cover the head of a metal hammer with a cloth. A gauge can be made (see diagram) and plastic guides are available to buy, but they are not very helpful.

A gadget made from metal is a useful guide for accurate close nailing. These have to be made specially, as only plastic ones are available to purchase. The cantilevered handle lets you get a grip, while the nail is hammered home.

Attaching a nail strip

Nail strip is available in yard (meter) length strips in either a bronze or a brass finish, with matching domed nails. Each strip has 10 holes for the domed nails.

1 Holding the strip in one hand, place a domed nail in the first hole and hammer it home. Take special care if you're using a metal hammer instead of a rubber-tipped one.

2 Repeat this on subsequent holes.

3 Where the strips need joining then overlap two holes.

Nails with a decorative domed head (as seen, left) can be used individually to anchor fabric instead of tacks and gimp or braid.

4 Hammer a nail through the two holes to complete the join.

Types of furniture

A variety of different chairs and sofas—from traditional to modern—are featured in this section together with a description of their upholstery, a list of the materials used, a cutting plan, and a comprehensive calculation of the amount of fabric you will require for each piece. Instruction on how to measure the different components is also included.

How to use cutting plans

First, use a soft tape measure to calculate the components needed to re-cover the chair. Record these on a chart. The measurements given on the following pages are only estimates and should, therefore, be used simply as a guide. When all the measurements have been recorded, transfer them to a cutting plan. The total figure at the bottom of the left-hand column is the amount of fabric required.

For more information on how to use cutting plans see page 92. The abbreviations used in this section are explained on page 9.

Dining chairs
Edwardian chair with a drop-in seat

DINING CHAIR VARIATIONS

Wooden seat frame with solid plywood base This is the ideal beginner's project. Decide what density foam you'd like, then use a spray adhesive to put a layer of bonded poly on top. Finally, stretch the cover over and attach with staples or tacks.

Seat with serpentine springs Following the plans laid out in this book, put on the layers of padding, then muslin, and the final fabric covering. You don't have to stick to traditional fabrics—use whatever strikes your fancy.

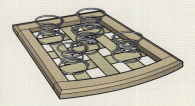

Drop-in seat with coil springs This is a lot like the seat with serpentine springs, but purists would tend to keep the fabric on this one traditional.

The Edwardian dining chair, introduced in the early 1900s, was usually made from beech or oak and stained to look like mahogany, walnut, or rosewood. The chairs were often reproductions of the Victorian period, mass produced and upholstered traditionally.

Anatomy

The drop-in seat is an ideal project for the beginner. The seat can be removed from the chair—where it fits neatly into the chair rails—so it is an easily transportable project. Upholstering the drop-in seat teaches the beginner the rudiments of upholstery, webbing, attaching burlap, and basic hair stuffing. The webbing is attached to the top of the frame to form a base for the burlap. Bridles are stitched onto the burlap to hold the stuffing of hair, coir, or black fiber, and then covered with a layer of white cotton batting and muslin. The muslin is stretched tightly over the hair and tacked on the underside of the frame. Then the black platform fabric is tacked to the underneath of the frame to cover the raw edges and tacks. Occasionally chairs have short coil springs in the base. Modern chairs can have serpentine springs, or on very basic chairs, a base of plywood. In these cases, use foam or rubberized hair to upholster.

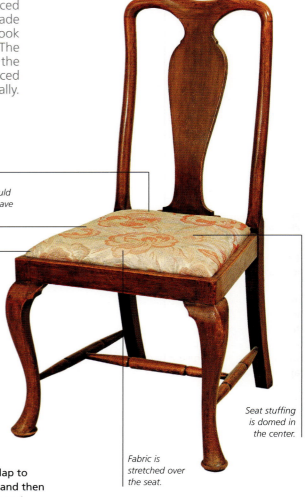

Weave is straight from front to back and side to side.

Stuffing on sides should be smooth and not have any lumps.

Neatly pleated corners.

Seat stuffing is domed in the center.

Fabric is stretched over the seat.

❏ SEE ALSO
Webbing, page 40; Preparing a burlap base, page 58; First stuffings, page 68.

Dining chairs   119

Thumbnail guide for taking measurements

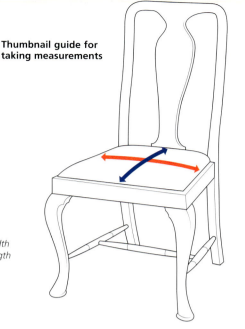

✳ UPHOLSTERER'S TIP
When attaching muslin to drop-in seats, keep the sides free of any stuffing so that the frame will fit into the chair when finished.

components	Length in.	cm	Width in.	cm	number required
SEAT	22	56	24	61	1

KEY
⎯⎯ = Width
⎯⎯ = Length

Fabric required

Plain or patterned fabric for 1 or 2 chairs: 2 ft. (0.6 m)
Plain or patterned fabric for 3 or 4 chairs: 3.9 ft. (1.2 m)

Extra material may be required for the 3 or 4 chairs to be identical. Upholstery fabric is normally 54 in. (137 cm) wide.

Measure the seat from underneath the rail at the back and front, and from side to side. A remnant of fabric is ideal for one chair as it is sometimes only possible to buy fabric by the yard. Buying fabric becomes more economical when covering multiple seats—the width of the purchased fabric will generally be enough for two seats, and approximately 3.9 ft. (1.2 m) will cover four seats.

If the fabric has a large pattern, place it in the center of the chair and cut two identical pieces from the width. When there are four or more seats, consider the placement of the pattern on the chair.

Total: 2 ft./ 0.6 m

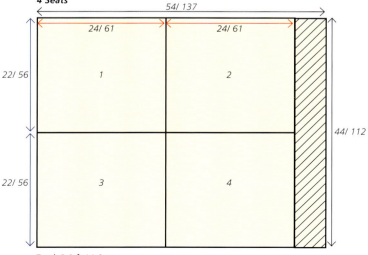

Total: 3.9 ft./ 1.2 m

Centralize these pieces if using a large-patterned fabric.

Stuffed over-seats
Balloon-back stuffed over-seats

STUFFED OVER-SEAT VARIATIONS

Stuffed over-seat piano stool This design would suit a cream trellis-weave textile.

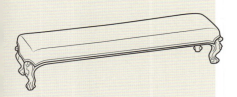

Prayer stool (note the sloping angle of the stool for kneeling on). Usually covered in leather, for long-lasting wear. Seen in smaller, much older churches in needlepoint, sometimes displaying parishioners' names.

Round piano stool This piece turns in both directions to go higher or lower and usually comes with claw feet. Also could be used as a dressing table stool.

A Victorian balloon-back dining chair has a stuffed over-seat and is upholstered using traditional materials and methods.

Fabric stretched over chair

Corners without a pleat

Gimp covering raw edges of fabric

Small pattern centered

Fabric tucked into corner

Anatomy

An upholstered stuffed over-seat, like the Victorian balloon-back dining chair, has many of the basic principles of traditional upholstery and is a good project for the beginner. It is easily transportable and will provide the beginner with the skills to advance to bigger projects. The seat has a webbed base covered with burlap, rather than springs. The first stuffing and stitched edge are of hair or fiber, and the second stuffing is normally of hair. These stuffings are covered with white cotton batting and muslin before the top fabric is added. The top fabric is stapled down to the show wood frame, and two tulip style pleats finish the rounded corners. The fabric is trimmed close to the show wood, and the raw edges are covered with a gimp or braid attached with a hot-glue gun. The chair's underside should only be covered with a barrier cloth if there are tack marks to be concealed.

❏ SEE ALSO
Webbing, page 40; First stuffings, page 68; Stitching an edge, page 80; Second stuffings, page 86; Attaching new coverings, page 94; Finishing the chair, page 112.

Stuffed over-seats

components	Length in.	cm	Width in.	cm	number required
SEAT	26	66	27	68	1

❋ UPHOLSTERER'S TIP
If you are only covering one chair, check to see if a fabric shop has a remnant for sale— this will be enough to do the job and cheaper than buying a whole yard.

Thumbnail guide for taking measurements

KEY
— = Width
— = Length

Fabric required

Plain fabric for 1 or 2 chairs:
2.3 ft. (0.7 m)
Plain fabric for 3 or 4 chairs:
4.5 ft. (1.5 m)
Patterned fabric for 1 or 2 chairs:
3 ft. (1 m)
Patterned fabric for 3 or 4 chairs:
6.6 ft. (2 m)

The measurements of an average-size stuffed overseat are: length 26 in. (66 cm) and width 27 in. (68 cm). Fabric is (usually) 54 in. (137 cm) wide, so two seats can be cut from one width of fabric. If the seat requires more than 27 in. (68 cm), then only one can be cut from the width. The cutting plans indicate the fabric required for up to four chairs with both plain and patterned fabric. It is more economical to buy fabric for a multiple of chairs rather than single ones. Choose patterned fabric with a centered pattern. If the chair has show wood at the front and sides, use a matching gimp to cover the raw edge of fabric.

1 Chair

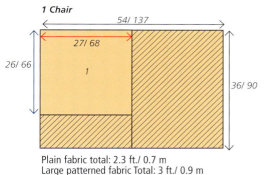

Plain fabric total: 2.3 ft./ 0.7 m
Large patterned fabric Total: 3 ft./ 0.9 m

4 Chairs

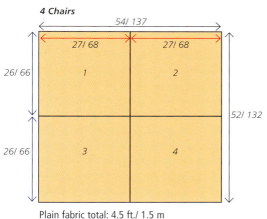

Plain fabric total: 4.5 ft./ 1.5 m
Large patterned fabric Total: 6.6 ft./ 2 m

2 Chairs

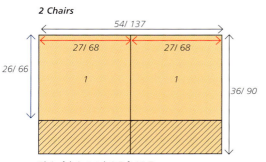

Plain fabric total: 2.5 ft./ 0.7 m
Large patterned fabric total: 3 ft./ 0.9 m

Armchairs
Small Victorian armchair

ARMCHAIR VARIATIONS

Small winged chair This great little chair works in areas that are challenging due to lack of space. You can upholster it to fit in with the existing room style.

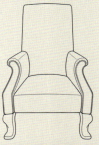

Wooden seat frame with solid plywood base This has a mahogany frame covered in leather. This is a chair that will be re-covered many times in its life.

Early Victorian armchair This elegant seat has a cord above the lumber part of the back and fringing at the front.

This small and traditionally upholstered armchair has tapered front legs and deep buttoned arms.

Stitched roll on the top joining up with the arms

Deep buttons on arms

Covered buttons

Welt at the bottom edge

Contrasting fabric welted edge

Anatomy

This Victorian armchair has a fully upholstered seat, back, and arms. The seat is sprung with nine coil springs on a webbed base. It has two stuffings of hair and a deep, firm, stitched edge at the front. The back has no springs, but two stuffings of hair and a stitched roll on the top edge. White cotton batting and muslin cover the stuffings of hair on the seat and the back, the muslin being tightly stretched and tacked down. Since the chair is narrow, the arms have only a thin stuffing of hair and a covering of white cotton batting and muslin. The top of the arms has a stitched edge and the top cover has three deep buttons that take the fabric around the arm's curve. The roll on the arms joins up with the roll on the top of the back.

❏ SEE ALSO
Webbing, page 40; Springing, page 46; Preparing a burlap base, page 58; First stuffings, page 68; Stitching an edge, page 80; Second stuffings, page 86; Attaching new coverings, page 94; Deep buttoning, 98; Making single and double welt, 106.

Armchairs 123

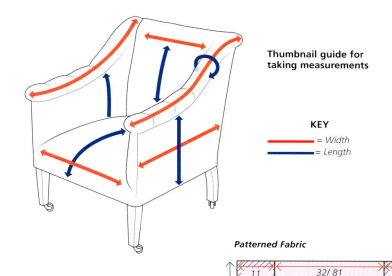

Thumbnail guide for taking measurements

KEY
— = Width
— = Length

components	Length in.	cm	Width in.	cm	number required
SEAT	32	81	32	81	1
I. BACK	30	76	25	63	1
O. BACK	24	61	25	63	1
I. ARM	26	66	29	74	2
O. ARM	24	61	27	68	2
TOP OF ARM	12	30	39	99	2

Fabric required

Plain fabric: 11.5 ft. (3.5 m)
Patterned fabric: 13.5 ft. (4.1 m)

Use a plain or small patterned fabric for this chair, since a large pattern would be lost on the small inside arms and in the deep buttoning on the arms. The pictured chair has welt made from a check fabric that has been cut on the bias. It's tacked to the frame, and the top fabric is slip stitched to it. The welt along the bottom of the chair is tacked on the underneath of the frame and dustcover fabric covers the raw edges. Allow extra fabric for the sloping angle on the width of the arms. The fabric on the top of the arm can be taken from the length or width, depending on the pattern. Allow 20 in. (0.5 m) extra fabric for the welt when using patterned fabric.

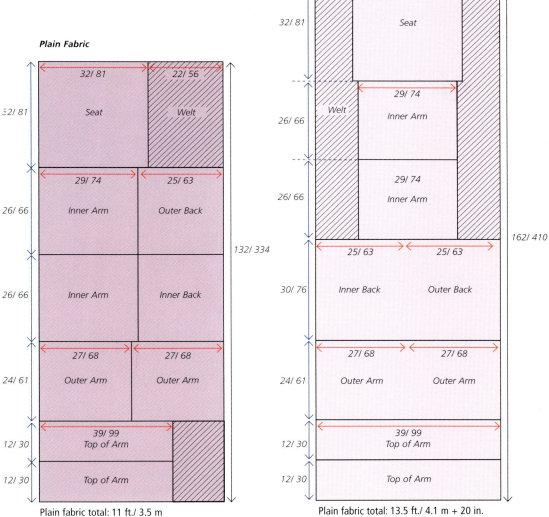

Armchairs
Victorian spoon-back chair

> ❋ Upholsterer's Tip
> Buttons made by an upholsterer on a buttoning machine are highly preferable to those made from a purchased kit. Button fabric can be obtained from off-cuts from the seat.

ARMCHAIR VARIATIONS

Ladies chair with cabriole legs This deep-buttoned, armless chair enabled a lady to sit to arrange her petticoats. This 19th-century piece is an elegant classic.

Spoon-back chair with plain back Also known as an "elbow chair," this can be used at the dining table.

Spoon-back chair with deep-buttoned back This mid-19th century piece usually comes with lovely carved details on arms, legs, and top of back.

This oak-framed Victorian armchair has a sprung seat and deep-buttoned arms and back.

- Buttons on back in diamond pattern
- Third button on arm hides join in fabric
- Carving of oak leaf on top of arm
- Braid attached just above show wood
- Carved and stout legs indicate a chair's high quality
- Angle of back legs indicates superior quality

Anatomy

Coil springs are stitched to the webbing base and covered with burlap and two stuffings of hair. There is a stitched edge at the front and a covering of white cotton batting and muslin prior to the top cover. The deep-buttoned back is formed with a thick layer of hair on a burlap base with a stitched edge all around; this gives the back a definite shape. White cotton batting and polyester batting cover the back, and a stitched edge around the carved show wood details the arms. The outside back and arms are covered with burlap and the top cover. A glued-on gimp or braid covers the raw edges on the front and back.

Armchairs

❏ **SEE ALSO**
Webbing, page 40; Springing, page 46; Working a sprung edge, page 54; Preparing a burlap base, page 58; First stuffings, page 68; Stitching an edge, page 80; Second stuffings, page 86; Attaching new coverings, page 94; Deep buttoning, 98; Finishing the chair, page 112.

Thumbnail guide for taking measurements

KEY
— = Width
— = Length

components	Length in.	cm	Width in.	cm	number required
SEAT	32	81	32	81	1
I. BACK	40	102	32	81	1
O. BACK	34	86	30	76	1
I. ARM	26	66	24	61	2
O. ARM	16	41	20	51	2

Fabric required

10.5 ft. (3.2 m) plain fabric
12.8 ft. (3.9 m) patterned fabric

Work out the fabric by imagining the chair flat. The pile of the fabric should go from top to bottom, on the seat from back to front, and on the arms from the top of the arm down to the seat. Allow extra fabric for the buttoned area—1.5 in. (4 cm) per button. Use seven pattern pieces to cover the chair. Fold the arm fabric over the back fabric at the back of the arm, and secure it with a button. Slip stitch the outside arm to the outside back down the line of the back rails. Because of the deep buttoning and the size of the seat, you will need extra material for a large patterned fabric. Stripes and large patterns become distorted with the buttoning, so an all-over random pattern is recommended.

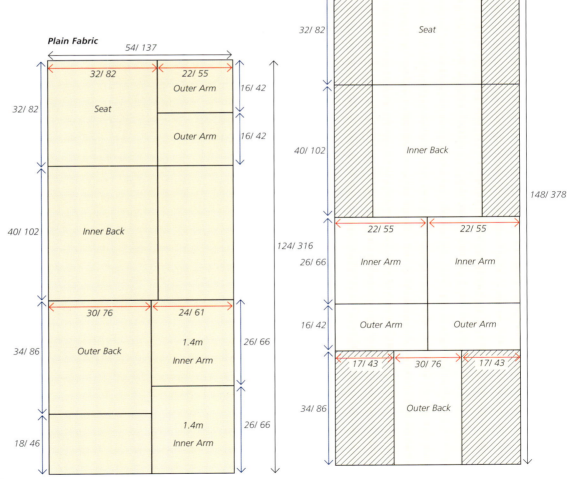

The components for the arms on the cutting plan for patterned fabric are cut larger in width to allow the pattern to be centralized.

Plain fabric total: 10.5 ft./ 3.2 m

Patterned fabric total: 12.8 ft./ 3.9 m

Armchairs
Victorian horseshoe chair

✻ Upholsterer's Tip
Use a hot-glue gun and clear glue stick to glue braid or gimp to the chair. The glue dries rapidly, so have tools ready and work quickly, gluing a small length at a time.

ARMCHAIR VARIATIONS

Horseshoe chair with curved back Castors allow the chair to roll smoothly. Look for a cream velour or green leather, to show off the rosewood legs.

Horseshoe chair with curved buttoned back and seat A buttoner's dream, this piece is ordinarily covered in leather. It's perfect for a pub, club, library, family room, or den.

Horseshoe chair with upholstered back and arms Another one for a leather cover, although don't restrict yourself to black. Make sure the show wood is clean and polished, and the nails properly spaced and aligned.

The Victorian horseshoe chair, or library chair, has a sprung seat, a curved, deep-buttoned back, and upholstered arms.

- Decorative cord covers stitching
- Buttons symmetrically positioned
- Arm and back slip stitched together
- Gimp hides tacked edge
- Fully sprung seat with stitches at front
- Neatly pleated corners.
- Gimp around front

Anatomy

The horseshoe chair comes in several slightly different styles. The style shown above has a coil sprung seat and a stuffing of hair, white cotton batting, and muslin with a stitched edge along the front edge. The back has a stitched edge around the two scroll ends and along the top of the back, which gives it its shape. It has seven deep buttons. The stitched edge on the arms stabilizes the stuffing and gives the arms shape. When upholstering, take care to make the arms of the chair identical. Instead of welt, decorative cord is stitched on the back's scroll ends. The raw edges of fabric at the front and arms are covered with gimp, which is glued on using a hot-glue gun.

❑ SEE ALSO
Webbing, page 40; Springing, page 46; First stuffings, page 68; Stitching an edge, page 80; Second stuffings, page 86; Attaching new coverings, page 94; Finishing the chair, page 112.

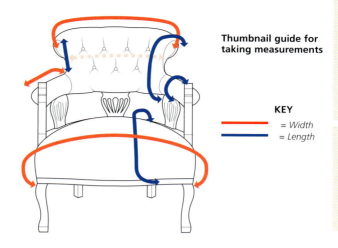

Thumbnail guide for taking measurements

KEY
— = Width
— = Length

✻ UPHOLSTERER'S TIP
When you upholster the arms, use two pieces of muslin the same size to make the arms identical.

✻ UPHOLSTERER'S TIP
Use extra material if you plan to make welt instead of using a decorative cord.

components	Length in.	cm	Width in.	cm	number required
SEAT	36	92	38	96	1
I. BACK	28	72	28	71	1
O. BACK	10	26	20	50	1
ARMS	10	26	18	46	2
FACINGS	8	20	6	15	2

Fabric required

5.6 ft. (1.7 m) plain or patterned fabric

Large patterned fabric is not ideal for the Victorian horseshoe chair because of the deep buttoning and narrow arms. Instead, use fabric with a self or small asymmetrical pattern. The chair has seven fabric components: the seat, inside back, outside back, arms, and two facings. To figure out which way the fabric should go on the arms, imagine the chair is flat. You will see that the length of the fabric goes from top to bottom and the width from side to side—as the diagram shows. The fabric on the arm is slip-stitched to the back fabric. The fabric on the scroll end is stuffed with batting and slip-stitched into place.

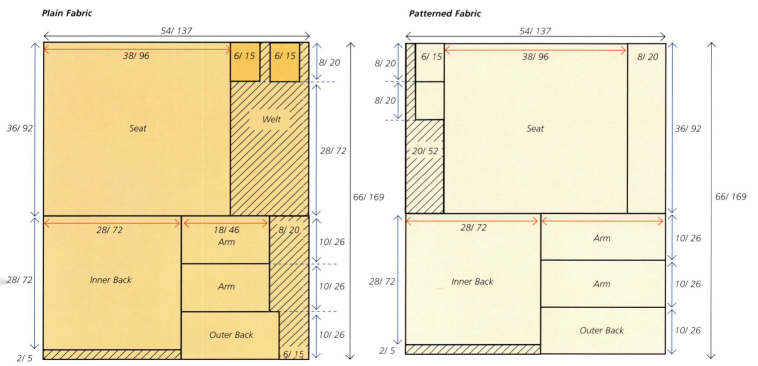

Plain fabric total: 5.6 ft./ 1.7 m

Patterned fabric total: 5.6 ft./ 1.7 m + extra 20 in. (0.5 m) if welting required.

Bedroom armchairs
Modern bedroom chair

BEDROOM CHAIR VARIATIONS

Modern bedroom chair with upholstered seat and back Contemporary in style, but works as an all-purpose chair. Uses clean lines with no frills. Perfect as additional seating.

Bedroom chair with curved seat and shaped back From the Art-Deco period, this piece has an overstuffed seat and three-channeled back. At home at a dressing table.

Slipper chair This piece has no arms and works with or without a loose seat cushion. It nicely shows off the woodwork of the legs and also gives a sense of space, as you "look through" the chair.

This chair is upholstered with foam or rubberized hair and has a box-pleated skirt. It's covered with a check fabric.

Back tacking strip

Seat fabric stretched tightly

Box pleats

Anatomy

Modern materials make up the upholstery on this basic chair. However, rubber webbing and foam do not have a long life span; replace them after a few years. Rubber webbing is used as the base and is stapled to the top of the frame. In better quality chairs the rubber webbing has metal fixing-clips attached to the ends, which fit into slots on the top of the seat frame. Fire-retardant foam and a protective layer of polyester batting cover the webbing. Muslin is stretched over the webbing, which helps to take the pressure off the top fabric. The top fabric is tacked or stapled to the outside edge of the seat frame. The skirt is either gathered or pleated and is made up prior to attaching. It is then back tacked onto the side rail of the chair.

❏ SEE ALSO
Webbing, page 40; Springing, page 46; Stitching an edge, page 80; Preparing a burlap base, 58; Second stuffings, page 86; Attaching new coverings, page 94.

Bedroom armchairs

components	Length in.	cm	Width in.	cm	number required
SEAT	26	66	26	66	1
I. BACK	28	71	27	68	1
O. BACK	24	61	22	56	1
VALANCE PLEATED	14	36	108	274	1

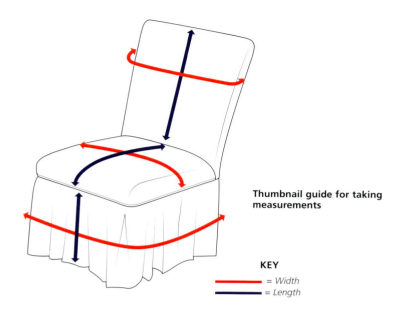

Thumbnail guide for taking measurements

KEY
— = Width
— = Length

Fabric required

6.6 ft. (2 m) plain or patterned fabric

If using check fabric on this chair, cut the welt on the bias. Attach the seat and back with staples or tacks, and tack the outside back on the top. Slip stitch down the sides. Line the skirt with curtain lining or muslin, which you need to make up before attaching. This includes the welt, which is machine-stitched to the top edge of the skirt. Measure the circumference of the chair and make the skirt to fit. The cutting plan allows for double the measurement of the circumference of the chair for the valance.

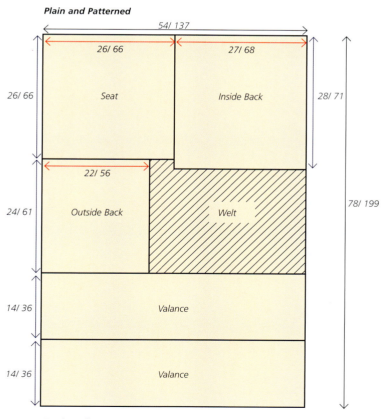

Winged armchairs
Modern winged fireside chair

✴ **UPHOLSTERER'S TIP**
When you insert a zipper in a cushion, always take the zipper around the back corners to make inserting the cushion pad easier. Make a pocket in which the zipper end can go by cutting the cushion wall longer than the required length.

WINGED CHAIR VARIATIONS

Modern rocker chair with loose seat cushion This chair looks good in any covering: dress it up in a classic paisley; toughen it up in leather; playful in plaid.

Modern upholstered wing chair with skirt The perfect place for grandma to read to her small grandchild.

Modern wing chair with curved wings and curved front facings This piece has a buttoned back to sink into, and will always look good covered in a duck egg soft blue-green.

Modern upholstery methods are used for this winged fireside chair.

Welting on the wings cut on the bias.

Edge or tack roll around outline of arms and wings

The upholsterer thought it would be fun to re-upholster this winged chair in a patchwork of co-ordinating textiles. The cutting plan (opposite) assumes that you will be working with a single length of fabric.

Welted edge at top and bottom of cushion

Loose box cushion made of foam

Edge or tack roll around seat front.

Welted edge to front facings

Anatomy

This winged armchair dating from around 1940 has been upholstered using rubberized hair rather than real hair, coir, or fiber. This is covered by a layer of wool and cotton batting, muslin, and then the top fabric. Coil springs have been used on the seat and back. Staples have been used throughout instead of tacks. There are no stitched edges but an edge, or tack roll, has been used to form a foundation along the front edge of the seat, and around the edge of the arms and wings. The cushion is made of foam and the cushion cover has a zipper that is positioned at the back of the cushion and extends round both back corners for ease of inserting the cushion pad.

❏ SEE ALSO
Springing, page 46; Preparing a burlap base, page 58; First stuffings, page 68; Stitching an edge, page 80; Second stuffings, page 86; Attaching new coverings, page 94, Making box cushions, page 108.

Winged armchairs 131

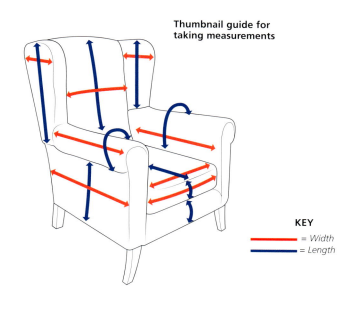

Thumbnail guide for taking measurements

KEY
— = Width
— = Length

components	Length in.	cm	Width in.	cm	number required
I. BACK	36	91	27	68	1
O. BACK	30	76	27	68	1
I. ARM	22	56	27	69	2
O. ARM	14	36	24	61	2
I. WING	20	51	14	36	2
O. WING	18	46	12	31	2
CUSHION	24	61	22	56	2
CUSHION WALL 1	5	13	54	137	1
2	6	15	54	137	1
FRONT FACING	12	31	36	91	1
ARM FACING	18	46	8	20	2

Fabric required

11.5 ft. (3.5 m) plain fabric
13.5 ft. (4.1 m) patterned fabric

A hard-wearing fabric with a high rub test would be most suitable for this chair if it is to be well used. There are 17 fabric components, and if the fabric has a large pattern plan, cut it out carefully. An extra yard will ensure the pattern repeat can be centered. Make sure the weave of the fabric is vertical when applying all components (especially the inside and outside wings). The fabric on the back of the wing needs to line up with the outside arm. The T-shaped cushion has a welted edge top and bottom and a zipper at the back. Make a spring cover to cover the tension springs.

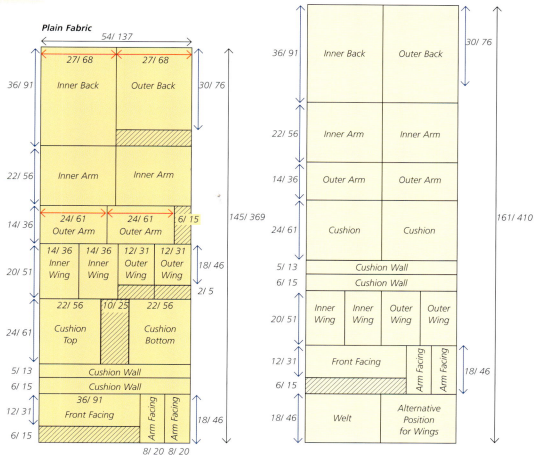

Plain fabric total: 12 ft./ 3.7 m

Patterned fabric total: 13.5 ft./ 4.1 m

Nursing chairs
Victorian nursing chair

✻ **Upholsterer's Tip**
When stitching a decorative cord use the blunt end of a small, curved needle to take the thread through the cord.

NURSING CHAIR VARIATIONS

Deep-buttoned nursing chair
A beautiful, classic piece of furniture. You don't need to be a nursing mother to appreciate the plush upholstery and comfortable fit.

Victorian nursing chair upholstered over bottom rail With its top to bottom channels, this one will test your upholstery skills, but it will be your reward to enjoy it.

Late Victorian nursing chair with fabric joined at the center and side facings
A lovely rolled back with sturdy base and legs makes this perfect in the bedroom—graceful and comfy.

This small nursing chair has a curved seat. The fabric on the back is in three pieces and is joined underneath the cord.

Fabric joined here

Scroll edges at top and bottom

Cord glued to hide tacks

Outside back stitched to welt

Brass finials covering screws

Decorative cord used instead of piping

Anatomy

The seat and the back of this chair are made from one piece of fabric. The curve of the chair makes it difficult to tighten the top fabric without any creases. The chair can be buttoned with either deep or shallow buttoning, or two vertical rows of stitching; the stitching hidden with a decorative cord. The stuffing on the sides of the chair is stitched into a small roll using a large curved needle instead of a long double pointed one. The seat is upholstered without springs. The outside-back welt is stapled on both sides. The fabric at the top is carded and slip stitched to the welt, and then tacked onto the bottom rail. The underneath of the chair can be covered with a colored decking or a scrap of available fabric.

❏ SEE ALSO
Webbing, page 40; Preparing a burlap base, page 58; First stuffings, page 68; Stitching an edge, page 80; Second stuffings, page 86; Attaching new coverings, page 94; Making single and double welt, page 106; Finishing the chair, page 112.

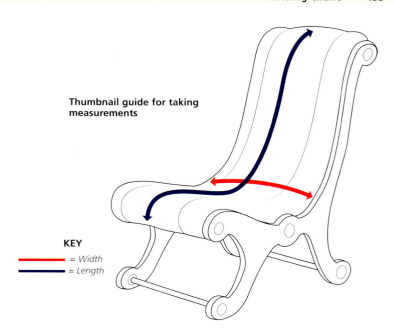

Thumbnail guide for taking measurements

KEY
— = Width
— = Length

components	Length in.	cm	Width in.	cm	number required
FRONT	46	117	20	51	1
O. BACK	22	56	15	38	1

Fabric required

4 ft. (1.2 m) plain or patterned fabric

The same amount of fabric is required whether it is plain or patterned, but because the chair is narrow, a plain or small pattern is advisable. Use only two pieces of fabric for this chair, which can be cut from the width of the fabric. The length used for the seat determines the amount of fabric you will need, and off-cut pieces of welt can be used. Stitch two vertical rows and tighten the fabric down the center so there are no creases. Tack or staple the side pieces onto the frame next to the show wood. Use extra fabric if the chair is to be deep buttoned, allowing ½ in. (13 mm) extra between each button on width and length. Glue decorative cord onto the raw edges of fabric.

❋ UPHOLSTERER'S TIP
If using a patterned fabric on this chair, it is advisable to use a small, random pattern so that the joins are not obvious.

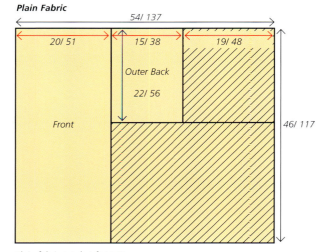

Plain fabric total: 4 ft./ 1.2 m

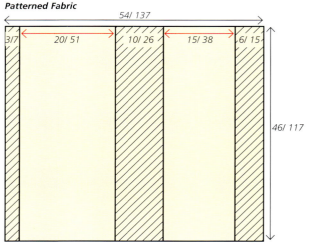

Patterned fabric total: 4 ft./ 1.2 m

Wood frames
Pin-cushion seats and backs

WOOD FRAME VARIATIONS

Stool or window seat This seat from the mid-18th century, requires a very thin padded cushion. It is a piece that can fit anywhere: at your dressing table, piano, or at the foot of the bed.

Chair back This Art-Nouveau piece would suit contemporary fabric selections. The chair would serve you well in hall or conservatory.

Folding chair Add a pin-cushion chair pad and take the chair outside—to the beach, the park, wherever. Casual is the attitude.

A pin-cushion seat has a very thin layer of padding on the top of the frame and is finished off with gimp or braid.

Corners without a pleat

Fabric smooth at sides

Braid attached to hide raw edges

Anatomy

A wood-frame chair with a pin-cushion seat is another ideal project for the beginner. The base of the seat can be a piece of plywood or a frame that needs webbing. Before you upholster, note where the black decking was attached. If there are no tack marks underneath the chair, then the black fabric would have been on the top of the frame, so attach this first.

If there are marks underneath, then the black fabric is added last. If the black fabric is to go on the top, anchor it first with a few tacks followed by webbing, burlap, a thin layer of hair, white cotton batting, and muslin. When you tighten the muslin, make sure the edges have a smooth slope so there is no necessity for a pleat at the corners.

❏ SEE ALSO
Webbing, page 40; First stuffings, page 68; Attaching new coverings, page 94; Finishing the chair, page 112.

Wood frames

components	Length in.	cm	Width in.	cm	number required
SEAT	21	53	21	53	1

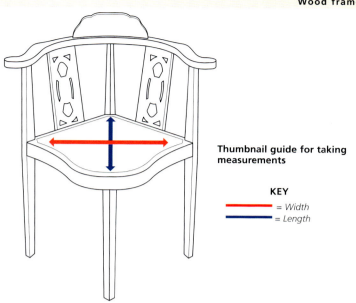

Thumbnail guide for taking measurements

KEY
— = Width
— = Length

Fabric required

Plain or patterned fabric for 1 or 2 chairs: 2 ft. (0.6 m)
Plain or patterned fabric 3 or 4 chairs 3.6 ft. (1.1 m)

Extra material may be required if the pattern match is large and an identical pattern is required on each seat. Measure from the back of the seat to the front, and from one side to the other. If the seat is small, it may be possible to cut the fabric for three seats from one width.

When using patterned fabric, cut extra so the pattern can be centered on the seat. With a corner chair, the fabric will run from the back corner to the front corner; it's best to use a larger piece of fabric because of the raw edges on the cross weave of the fabric, and to accommodate for stretching. To prevent stretching, temporarily tack the corners and then the center of the sides, gradually working out to the corners. Measure around the four sides of the seat to work out how much braid or gimp is required, adding two inches for turnings. Then make the join of the braid or gimp at the back corner with the two ends of braid or gimp butted together.

1–2 Chairs

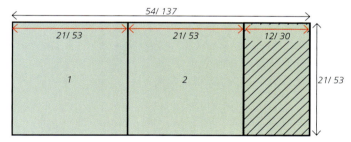

Total: 2 ft./ 0.6 m

4 Chairs

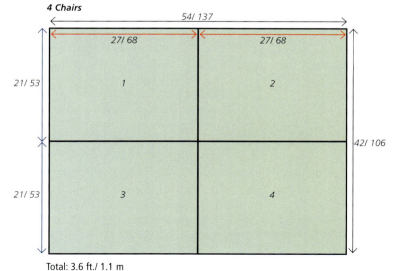

Total: 3.6 ft./ 1.1 m
Components centralized when using patterned fabric.

Wood frames
Modern chair with wooden frame

WOOD FRAME VARIATIONS

Modern chair with curved back and arm rail This chair is similar to a modern mid-20th century boardroom chair. Perfect with green leather.

Modern chair with two cushions and arm pads This is a great chair for the library, which would best suit a tapestry fabric.

Modern chair with round seat and upholstered back pad This contemporary style is best used in commercial settings, such as conference and meeting rooms. Would suit leather or vinyl.

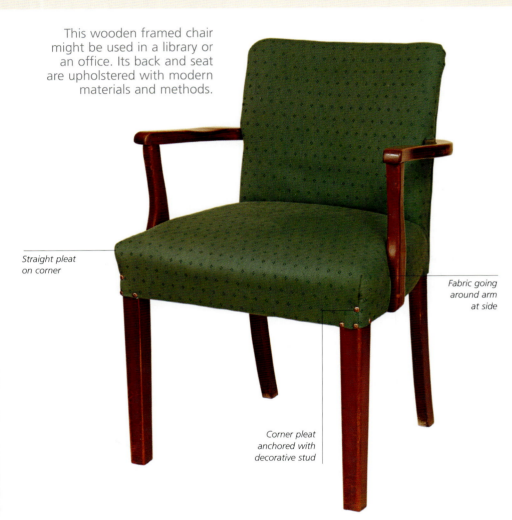

This wooden framed chair might be used in a library or an office. Its back and seat are upholstered with modern materials and methods.

Straight pleat on corner

Fabric going around arm at side

Corner pleat anchored with decorative stud

Anatomy

The seat's serpentine springs are anchored to the chair frame with clips and nails. These are covered with burlap and a piece of 2 in. (5 cm) rubberized hair, cut to the shape of the seat. The rubberized hair is secured to the burlap using a spray adhesive. Blue batting and white cotton batting are placed on top of the sheet of hair and trimmed away to cover the rough edge of the hair. A tight covering of muslin over the batting is anchored to the underside of the chair with Y-shaped cuts around the arms of the chair, and a diagonal cut into the back corners. The same procedure is used for the back, but with 1 in. (2.5 cm) rubberized hair. The top cover is anchored at the back, and the outside back is slip stitched on.

❏ SEE ALSO
Webbing, page 40; Springing, page 46; Preparing a burlap base, page 58; First stuffings, page 68; Attaching new coverings, page 94; Deep buttoning, 98.

Thumbnail guide for taking measurements

KEY
— = Width
— = Length

components	Length in.	cm	Width in.	cm	number required
SEAT	26	66	36	91	1
I. BACK	22	56	26	66	1
O. BACK	22	56	20	50	1

✲ **UPHOLSTERER'S TIP**
To create a smooth edge on top, chamfer the rubberized hair off the underneath edge.

Fabric required

4.3 ft. (1.3 m) plain or patterned fabric
20 in. (0.5 m) fabric for welt

The chair is covered with three pieces of fabric—the seat, inside back, and outside back. If the fabric is large-patterned, centralize it on the inside back and the seat. The fabric on the seat and inside back has a Y-cut around the arms, a diagonal cut at the back corners, and a straight pleat on the front and top corners. Card the outside back at the top and slipstitch down either side. Plain and large patterned fabric require the same amount of fabric, but extra may be required if the large pattern is to be centered on the seat and back. Extra material is required for welt as shown in cutting plan 2 (patterned fabric).

Plain Fabric

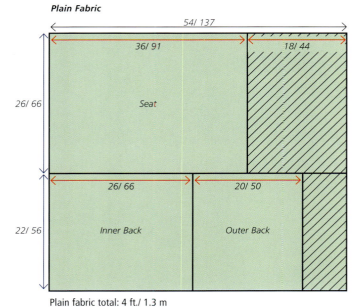

Plain fabric total: 4 ft./ 1.3 m

Patterned Fabric

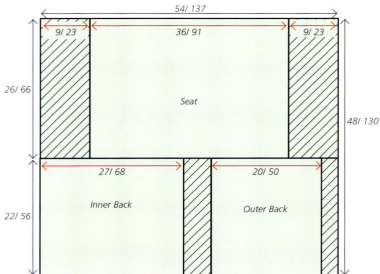

Patterned fabric total: 4 ft./ 1.3 m + 20 in. (0.5 m) welt if required

Settees
Modern two-seater settee

138 Types of furniture

❏ **SEE ALSO**
Webbing, page 40; Springing, page 46; Stitching an edge, page 80; Preparing a burlap base, 58; Second stuffings, page 86; Attaching new coverings, page 94; Making piping, page 106; Making a box cushion, page 108.

✳ **UPHOLSTERER'S TIP**
Use a hot-glue gun with a clear glue stick to glue braid or gimp to the chair. The glue is hot and dries quickly, so have your equipment on hand before starting.

SETTEE VARIATIONS

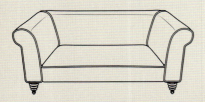

19th-century settee This pretty two-seater sofa with sturdy mahogany turned legs would have been upholstered traditionally and finished in a delicate brocade or silk fabric.

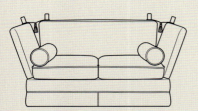

Knole settee The Knole settee originated in Kent in the early 18th century. This reproduction piece is made up of square-shaped frames, which are completely upholstered. It has two loose seat cushions and two bolsters. The hinged arms are held in place by decorative tasseled cords.

Modern Knole Settee The deep seat on this piece allows room for large throw pillows (scatter cushions). Use duck feathers in the single seat cushion. Leather is a fabulous covering on this timeless beauty.

This settee has been upholstered with modern methods and has four loose cushions with removable covers.

Back cushions shaped to sit on arm

Front facings machine-stitched with welt to arm piece

Welted edge to cushions

Fitted front facing

Anatomy

The frame of the settee is covered with a thin layer of stuffing so that the cushions are soft and comfortable. The settee is upholstered using serpentine springs on the seat with a covering of burlap and foam or rubberized hair. A layer of batting and a top cover complete the upholstery. The back and arms follow the same process, but without springs. The deep cushions have three sections filled with qualofil—a polyester fiber filling—which is very hard wearing. The sections prevent the cushion filling from moving inside the case. The zipper on the cushions goes along the back wall and several inches down either side. Save money by replacing the top fabric underneath the cushions on the seat and back with decking fabric. The fabric covering the settee is cotton with a fire-retardant backing.

components	Length in.	cm	Width in.	cm	number required
I. BACK	32	81	73	185	1
O. BACK	29	74	66	167	1
FRONT FACING	18	46	54	137	1
I. ARM	30	76	44	112	2
O. ARM	24	61	38	96	2
SEAT CUSHION	27	69	29	74	4
BACK CUSHION	20	51	35	89	4
SEAT WALLS	5	13	54	137	2
CUSHION	6	15	54	137	2
BACK CUSHION WALLS	5	13	54	137	2
	6	15	54	137	2

Settees

Fabric required

35 ft. (10.7 m) plain or patterned fabric

When using patterned fabric, decide where the pattern will be centralized on each of the components prior to cutting. The extra fabric allowed for welt gives flexibility, so use the cutting pattern as a guide rather than a fixed rule. Welt the large cushions on the seat and back with the same fabric as on the settee. Welt the front arm facings, also. All of the welt could be of a contrasting fabric, but make sure it is of a similar thickness as the chair fabric. Join the fabric where the width of the chair or settee is wider than the width of the fabric. Cut the extra length in two and add to either end of the large piece of fabric.

Thumbnail guide for taking measurements

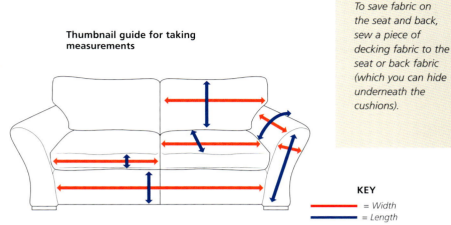

KEY
— = Width
— = Length

※ **UPHOLSTERER'S TIP**
To save fabric on the seat and back, sew a piece of decking fabric to the seat or back fabric (which you can hide underneath the cushions).

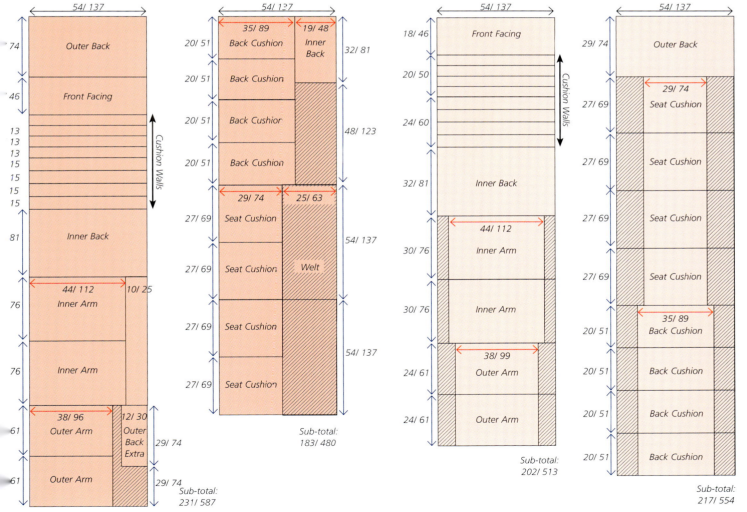

Plain fabric total: 35 ft./ 10.7 m

Patterned fabric total: 35 ft./ 10.7 m

Chaise longues
Traditional deep-buttoned chaise longues

CHAISE LONGUE VARIATIONS

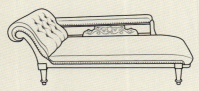

Edwardian chaise with buttoned head This type of chaise is sometimes described as being of inferior quality because of the simplicity of the carving and the somewhat narrow legs. It would have been filled with the cheapest stuffings and covered in a velvet or tapestry.

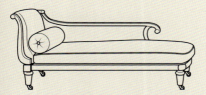

Regency-style chaise with bolster This type of chaise often only had a base of webbing and burlap covered by top fabric, and a thick squab cushion rather than a fully upholstered and sprung seat. The head has an inward-facing curve and a squab cushion to fit inside.

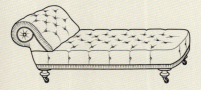

Day bed These were first introduced in the early 18th century together with chaise longues and were designed for lounging. This example has a deep-buttoned head and seat and would have been upholstered in a comfortable fabric, such as velvet or tapestry.

This comfortable 19th-century chaise longue with tapered legs and castors has deep buttoning on the back and head. There is a sprung edge around the seat, which may have been originally deep-buttoned in a velour, velvet, or damask.

Scroll end

Pattern of buttons following line of arm

Gathered border

Sprung edge all around seat

Decorative cord instead of welt

Anatomy

This chaise longue has a deep-buttoned, fully upholstered head and back, with no show wood. Horsehair is used as stuffing under the deep-buttoning, and a stitched edge runs along the top of the head and around the scroll-front facing. Another stitched edge runs along the top of the back to give the back its curved shape. As some of this roll is on a curve, it is best to use loose-weave scrim. The seat uses coil springs and has a sprung edge attached to a wire that runs around the seat to the back arm. This wire and stitched edge form a lip to which the muslin and top fabric is stitched. The border is gathered and slip-stitched to the underside of the lip. Decorative cord is then stitched on.

✷ **UPHOLSTERER'S TIP**
When deep buttoning, place a layer of polyester batting over the white cotton batting to stop cotton breaking up. To prevent a ridge forming around the button, cut a large hole in the polyester where the button is to go.

Chaise longues **141**

❏ SEE ALSO
Stripping, page 34; Webbing, page 40; Springing, page 46; Working a sprung edge, page 54; Preparing a burlap base, page 58; First stuffing, page 68; Stitching an edge, page 80; Second stuffing, page 86; Attaching new coverings, page 94; Making single and double welt, page 106; Finishing the chair, page 112.

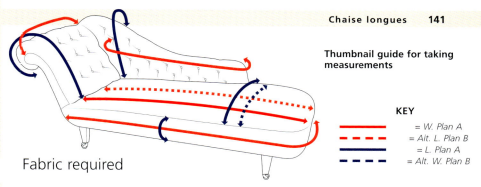

Thumbnail guide for taking measurements

KEY
— = W. Plan A
- - - = Alt. L. Plan B
— = L. Plan A
- - - = Alt. W. Plan B

Fabric required

components	Length in.	cm	Width in.	cm	number required
SEAT	38	97	71	180	1
ALTERNATIVE SEAT	71	180	38	97	1
I. ARM	40	102	106	268	1
O. ARM	28	72	54	137	1
I. BACK	54	138	45	114	1
O. BACK	24	61	30	76	1
BORDER	13	33	54	137	4

Cutting plan A: 25 ft. (7.5 m)
Cutting plan B: 26 ft. (7.9 m)

Before choosing a type of fabric, decide which way the fabric will go on the seat. **Cutting plan A** requires it to have a join. With **cutting plan B** the fabric runs the length of the seat. The pattern or pile of the fabric may determine the fabric's placement. If it's going to be joined, then it may be possible to tuck the join down between the back and seat.

Make sure that you have enough material. Take the widest points for any of the components' measurements and add on an extra 1.5 in. (3.8 cm) between each deep button. Allow enough fabric for all the tuck-ins needed—for example, the length will have to go through the gap between the seat and the back to the outside rail.

The fabric on the arm has a join which is best done through a button. Note that the width from the corner near the back to the end of the arm can be deceptive.

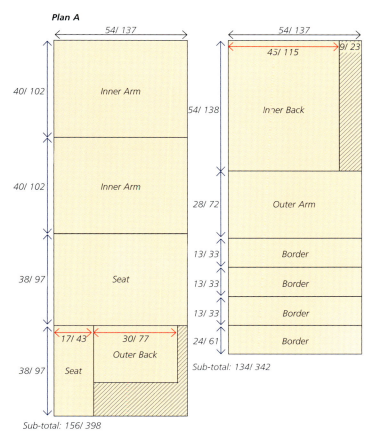

Plan A total: 25 ft./ 7.5 m

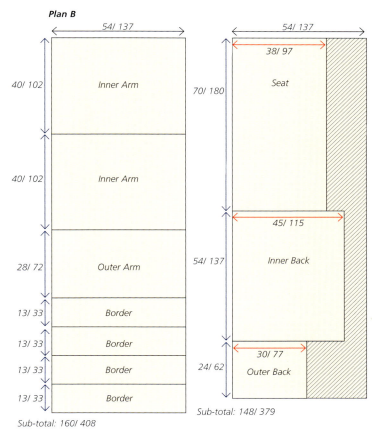

Plan B total: 26 ft./ 7.9 m

Index

A
acetate 27
acrylic 27
animal hair 20, 21, 68, 86, 87
   reusing 36
   traditional use of 10, 11
apron, upholstery 34
armchairs 122–31

B
backs
   pin-cushion 68, 134–5
   webbing 45
balloon-back stuffed overseats 120–2
balloon-backed chair, covering 94–5
barrier cloth 113
base fabric 94
batting 20, 21, 70, 86, 87
   polyester 98, 140
batting pad 34
bedroom armchairs 128–9
berry staple remover 37
black fiber 20, 21, 68
black and white webbing 17, 40
blind stitch 81–4
blue batting 20, 21
blue and white ticking 22
box cushions 108–11
braid 30, 112–13
bridles 69, 86–7
burlap 22, 58
burlap base 58–67
butterflies 98, 99, 104
buttoning
   deep 11, 98–102
   shallow 104–5
buttons, covered 98, 104, 124

C
camera 34
chairs
   stripping 34–5, 38
   see also armchairs; dining chairs; modern chairs; nursing chairs
chaise longues 140–1
chalk 46, 68, 114
Chesterfield 45
chisels 14, 34, 36
clips, for serpentine springs 46, 57
close nailing 114–15
coconut fiber 20, 21
coil springs 17, 46, 48
coir 20, 21, 68
color, fabric 26
contemporary styles 25
cord 18, 30, 46, 54
corners 73, 76, 77–9, 113
cotton batting 20, 21, 86, 87
cotton/cotton blends 27, 28
covered buttons 98, 104, 124
coverings 22–3
   attaching 94–7
   for first stuffings 70–3
curved needles 16, 58, 68, 86
cushions
   box 108–11
   pin-cushion seats and backs 68, 134–5
cut or blue tacks 18, 40
cutting plans 92–3, 117

D
decking 22
decorative braids 30, 112
decorative nails 18, 114
deep buttoning 11, 98–102
deep-buttoned chaise longue 140–1
dining chairs 118–21
double pointed needles 16, 68, 80, 98, 104
double welt 107
down-proof ticking 22
drop-in seats 40–1, 59–60, 68, 118–19
durability, of fabric 26

E
eclectic styles 25
edge rolls 67, 84–5
edge stitching 74, 80–5
edges, sprung 54–6, 64–6
Edwardian dining chair 118–19
elastic webbing 17, 40

F
fabrics 24–30
   attaching 58, 59, 60
   choosing 94
   grain 58, 88
   pile 92
   planning cuts 92–3
   tacking 94
face mask 34, 36
fade resistance 26
faux suede 28
feathers 20
fillings 20–1
finishing 112–13
fireside chair, winged 130–1
first stuffings 68–79
fixing bars 46
flat rail/flat curved arm, applying muslin 91
foam 20
frames, wood 118, 122, 134–7
   cleaning and repairing 39
front rail sprung edges 64–5
furniture
   findings and accessing 14
   types of 117–41

G
gimp 30, 112–13
gimp pins 18, 112, 113, 114
ginger coir 20, 21, 68
glove, used when stitching an edge 80–1
glue guns 112, 126, 138

H
hair see animal hair
hammers
   magnetic 14
   mallets 14, 34, 37
   rubber-tipped 114
horse hair see animal hair
horseshoe chair 126–7

J
joinings, fabric 103, 110, 111
jute webbing 17, 40

L
laid cord 18, 46, 54
leather 27, 28
linen 28
linings 22–3

M
magnetic hammer 14
mallets 14, 34, 37
materials 18–30
   modern 128
   previously used 35
   reusing 36
   traditional 10, 11
   see also tools and materials
measurement guides
   armchairs 123, 125, 127, 129, 131
   dining chairs 119, 121
   nursing chair 133
   settees and chaise longues 139, 141
   wood frame chairs 135, 137
measuring tips 71, 74, 87, 90, 93
metal plates 57
microfiber 27
mitered corners 113
modern chairs
   bedroom armchair 128–9
   stripping 36
   winged fireside chair 130–1
   with wooden frame 136–7
modern two-seater settee 138–9
muslin 22, 71–3, 76, 88–91

N
nail strips 18, 115
nailing, close 114–15
nails 18, 114
natural fabrics 27
needles 16
   for burlap base 58
   for buttoning 98, 104
   springing 46, 48, 69
   for stitching an edge 80
   for stuffing 68
notebook 34
nursing chairs 132–3
nylon 27

O
olefin 27
order of work 9
Osborne staple remover 37
overseats, stuffed 61–3, 120–1

P
patterned fabrics 93, 94–5, 101, 133
pile, of fabric 92
pincers 14, 34, 37
pincushion seats and backs 68, 134–5
piping/welt cord 18, 106
Pirelli webbing 17, 40
pleating 89, 100
polyester 27, 28
polyester batting 98, 140
protective gear 34, 36

R
railroad fabrics 93
rasp 68
rayon 27
record keeping 35, 117
regulators 16, 68, 80, 94, 98
ripping chisel 34
rubber-tipped hammer 114
rubberized hair 20, 21, 128

S
scissors 14
scrim 22
scroll gimp 30
seats
   dining chair variations 118
   overseat variations 120
   pin-cushion 68, 134–5
serpentine springs 17, 46, 57
settees 138–9
   webbing 45
sewing bridles 69, 86–7
sewing machine 106, 108
shallow buttoning 104–5
silk 27
silk blends 28
single welt 106–7
skewers 16, 98, 104
skin batting 20, 21
slipcover look 25
slipper chair 128
slipping thread 112
sloping side rail chair 96
slot and peg stretcher 14, 43–4
spade staple remover 37
spoon-back chairs 124–5
spring pads 57
spring units 47
springing 11, 46–57
springing needle 46, 58, 69
springs
   out of shape 36
   stitching burlap base to 63
   types of 17, 46–7, 48, 57
sprung edges 54–6, 64–6
square front legs 97
staple guns 14, 58, 94
staple removers 14, 34, 37, 58
staples 18, 46
stitched edges 74, 80–5
stitching
   to springs 63
   to webbing 49–50
stockinette 22
straight back legs 97
straight back rail chair 96
stretcher, slot and peg 14, 43–4
stripping 34–9
stuffed overseats 61–3, 120–1
stuffing techniques
   first stuffings 68–79
   second stuffings 86–91
stuffing ties 75
stuffings 20–1
   burlap as platform for 66
style, choosing 24–6
synthetic fabrics 27

T
tack removers 14, 34, 94
tacks
   for burlap base 58
   for coverings 94
   removing 36
   for springing 46, 54
   for stuffings 68, 76, 86
   types of 18
   for webbing 41
tailoring 26
tape measures 16
   measuring without 71, 87
techniques, traditional 10–11
   see also burlap base; buttoning; close nailing; covering; cutting plans; springing; sprung edges; stitching; stripping; stuffing; webbing; welt
tension springs 17, 46, 57
textiles 24–30
ticking 22
tools 12–17
tools and materials
   for box cushions 108
   for burlap base 58
   for buttoning 98, 104
   for close nailing 114
   for fabrics 92, 94
   for finishing 112
   for single/double welt 106
   for springing 46, 54
   for stitching an edge 80
   for stripping 34
   for stuffing 68, 86
   for vandyking 103
   for webbing 40
traditional deep-buttoned chaise longue 140–1
traditional styles 24
traditional techniques 10–11
transitional styles 24
trimmings 30–1
tulip pleat 89
twine 18, 46, 54, 68, 80
   nylon twine 98, 104
two-seater settee 138–9

U
upholstery apron 34

V
vandyking 103
velvet blends 28
Victorian armchairs 122–7
Victorian nursing chair 132–3
vinyl 27

W
wax chalk 16
webbing
   stitching to 49–50
   types of 10, 17, 40
webbing stretcher 14, 43–4
webbing techniques 40–5
welt, single and double 106–7
winged armchairs 122, 130–1
wire wool 34
wood frames see frames, wood
wooden mallets 14, 34, 37
wooden seat frame 118, 122
wool 27
wool blends 28
woollen batting 20, 21

Z
zippers 108, 110–11, 130

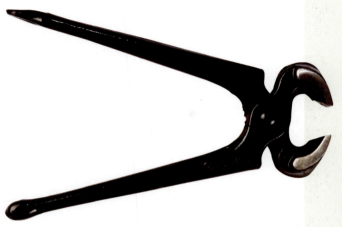

Credits

Photographs on pages 12, 32, 116-117 courtesy of Jane Churchill Fabrics & Wallpapers (copyright: Jane Churchill Fabrics & Wallpapers).

Pages 7, 13, 31, 33 courtesy of Osborne and Little (stocklist number +44 (0)20 7352 1456).

Page 25, photolibrary.com

Other photographs and illustrations are the copyright of Quarto Publishing plc. While every effort has been made to credit contributors, Quarto would like to apologize should there have been any omissions or errors—and would be pleased to make the appropriate correction for future editions of the book.

Quarto would also like to thank the following companies for supplying sample fabrics and tools:
Osborne and Little (www.osborneandlittle.com)
Nina Campbell (www.ninacampbell.com)
Laura Ashley (www.lauraashley.com)
Glover Bros., Taunton

US consultant
Patricia Gilkey, Second Chance Upholstery, a San Francisco Bay Area upholsterer for 20 years, vetted member and five-year Director of the Association of Master Upholsterers and Soft Furnishers, widely acknowledged as the trade association of the professionals.